ANALECTA GORGIANA

Volume 12

General Editor
George Anton Kiraz

Analecta Gorgiana is a collection of long essays and short monographs which are consistently cited by modern scholars but previously difficult to find because of their original appearance in obscure publications. Now conveniently published, these essays are not only vital for our understanding of the history of research and ideas, but are also indispensable tools for the continuation and development of on-going research. Carefully selected by a team of scholars based on their relevance to modern scholarship, these essays can now be fully utilized by scholars and proudly owned by libraries.

Evil as Explained in the Clementine and Lactantian Writings

Evil as Explained in the Clementine and Lactantian Writings

F. W. Bussell

Gorgias Press
2006

First Gorgias Press Edition, 2006

The special contents of this edition are copyright © 2006 by
Gorgias Press LLC

All rights reserved under International and Pan-American Copyright
Conventions. Published in the United States of America by
Gorgias Press LLC, New Jersey

This edition is a facsimile reprint of the
original edition titled "The Purpose of the World-Process and the Problem of
Evil as Explained in the Clementine and Lactantian Writings in a System of
Subordinate Dualism" published in *Studia Biblica et Ecclesiastica*,
Oxford, 1896, vol. 4.

Analecta Gorgiana pagination appears in square brackets.

ISBN 1-59333-490-7

GORGIAS PRESS
46 Orris Ave., Piscataway, NJ 08854 USA
www.gorgiaspress.com

The paper used in this publication meets the minimum requirements of the
American National Standards.

Printed in the United States of America

THE PURPOSE OF THE WORLD-PROCESS AND THE PROBLEM OF EVIL AS EXPLAINED IN THE CLEMENTINE AND LACTANTIAN WRITINGS IN A SYSTEM OF SUBORDINATE DUALISM.

F. W. BUSSELL

PART I.

GOD AS CREATOR AND JUDGE.

§ 1. IT may be boldly asserted that the main point at issue in the Ante-Nicene controversies and the Cardinal doctrine of the Fathers in the first three centuries, is the Personality of God, and His interest in the world. Even the subject of Incarnation and Redemption may be said for a time to be subordinate. 'Of what sort was the God whom Christ came to reveal?' By degrees the question assumed a different form, 'Is not the manifestation of the Divine Nature in Christ our only guide? "He that hath seen me hath seen the Father also"'. The world in its ceaseless interrogation of the historic Christ, passes through the same stages as Philip, believing that the Saviour came to preach an unknown Father, until convinced that not in some esoteric knowledge of the inscrutable, but in the life and character of Jesus lay the secret of the new revelation. In fact, in this announcement was a reaction against a then prevalent and mistaken reverence, in which lay a great peril to practical piety. In the religious world of both Greeks and Jews, and especially in that amalgam which united both, the divine conception had been gradually divested of character, affections, or titles

Subordinate Dualism.

in any way akin to mankind. In the end the Athenians had been right, on the assumption that they followed Plato and Aristotle. The unknown God was the only one which was left to them; an infinite sea of goodness, or an attenuated Final Cause. The Septuagint takes pains to respectfully correct those passages in the Old Testament which represent the Almighty as having bodily parts; as actuated by motives or swayed by affections which have their counterpart in man. PHILO JUDAEUS is always tending towards a neuter and impersonal notion of God (τὸ θεῖον, τὸ ὄν), as if attempting to separate and (perhaps) hypostatize all those qualities, characteristics, or actions in the Divine Being, on which the idea of *Providence* depends. 'God is after all unknowable; the divine word (θεῖος λόγος) is God in relation to us, so far as we can know Him and appreciate His manifestation;—His existence rather than His essence. It is this second God who has made the world[1], and presides over its destinies in the two spheres of Nature and History, even he perhaps not directly or by immediate contact, but through his principal powers, the Creative and the Kingly (ποιητική and βασιλική). Of these

---

[1] NUMENIUS, in EUSEBIUS, Pr. Ev. xi. 18 καὶ γὰρ οὔτε δημιουργεῖν ἐστὶ χρεὼν τὸν πρῶτον, καὶ τοῦ δημιουργοῦντος θεοῦ χρὴ εἶναι νομίζεσθαι πατέρα τὸν πρῶτον Θεόν . . . . ὁ θεὸς μέντοι ὁ δεύτερος καὶ τρίτος ἐστὶν εἷς· συμφερόμενος δὲ τῇ ὕλῃ δυάδι οὔσῃ ἑνοῖ μὲν αὐτήν, σχίζεται δὲ ὑπ' αὐτῆς . . . . καὶ ἀπερίοπτος ἑαυτοῦ γίνεται καὶ ἅπτεται τοῦ αἰσθητοῦ . . . . ὁ μὲν πρῶτος Θεὸς ἔσται ἑστὼς ὁ δὲ δεύτερος ἔμπαλίν ἐστι κινούμενος . . . . διομολογησώμεθα ἡμῖν αὐτοῖς ὁμολογίαν οὐκ ἀμφισβητήσιμον ἀκοῦσαι, τὸν μὲν πρῶτον Θεὸν ἀργὸν εἶναι ἔργων ξυμπάντων καὶ βασιλέα, τὸν δημιουργικὸν δὲ θεὸν ἡγεμονεῖν δι' οὐρανοῦ ἰόντα.

APOLLONIUS, in Eus. iv. 13. The First God δεῖται . . . . οὐδενὸς οὐδὲ παρὰ τῶν κρειττόνων ἥπερ ἡμεῖς, οὐδ' ἔστιν ὃ . . . . γῆ ἀνίησι φυτὸν ἢ τρέφει ζῷον ἢ ἀήρ, ᾧ μὴ πρόσεστί γέ τι μίασμα. The present creation, nay, man himself all but his innermost spiritual centre, was essentially contemptible in the eyes of these speculators of the Imperial age.—PLUTARCH, Is. et Os. § 78 ὁ δ' ἐστὶ μὲν αὐτὸς ἀπωτάτω τῆς γῆς ἄχραντος καὶ ἀμίαντος καὶ καθαρὸς οὐσίας ἁπάσης φθορὰν δεχομένης καὶ θάνατον. Ἀνθρώπων δὲ ψυχαῖς ἐνταυθοῖ μὲν ὑπὸ σωμάτων καὶ παθῶν περιεχομέναις οὐκ ἔστι μετουσία τοῦ Θεοῦ, πλὴν ὅσον ὀνείρατος ἀμαυροῦ θιγεῖν νοήσει διὰ φιλοσοφίας. The only way to this God was on the Path of Knowledge; He could not be approached by the practical life.—The gnostical idea of the Second God, the Creator, has been adopted from this system in Tennyson.

the former is wholly good and merciful (Nature), while the apparent asperity of the latter (History) is due to human sin, and represents not so much an essential attribute of the λόγος, as *our* altered relation to his uniform benevolence.'

The Epicurean deity, whose existence rested on the credit of dreams and survived only in deference to popular fanaticism (Epicurus had no intention of emulating the fate of Socrates or the confessorship of Anaxagoras),—this god, I say, had been long since conducted to the extreme limits of the known Universe, and forbidden to meddle with the course of the world, either in *natural* law (of which he was himself a manifestation) or in *human* history (to which he was entirely indifferent). The Stoics, with their habitual and unpardonable offence of retaining language which they laboured to deprive of all significance, are loud in their praises of the divine goodness, and subtle in their arguments on behalf of Providence; but it is a goodness which is purposeless, and a Providence which is unconscious. And it is only this poetic language of religious sentiment, which preserves the Stoics from the charge of atheism, or a blank admiration of physical force; of a certain steady equipoise or proportion in the Universe. It is also worthy of careful notice that those of the School who approach cosmogony from the *human* and the practical side, as SENECA and AURELIUS, ever tend to a half-Platonic Mysticism; which, so far from identifying the 'god within' and the course of the world without, leaves them in reality in irreconcilable opposition. Lastly, the Platonist, if I may be allowed to speak at this point of the later development of the third century, insists with singular earnestness upon the doctrine of necessary Sequence, natural concomitance, as against creation: not by the will of God (προαιρέσει) but (τῷ εἶναι) by Emanation does this universe, whether of thoughts or things, arise[1]. The Gnostic meantime

[1] The idea of deliberate creation in Greek philosophy is only found in the half-myth of the *Timaeus*. ARISTOTLE shifts the centre of gravity from

(against whose bitter discontent the genial optimism of Alexandria was to array its forces) involves the God and a Personal God to the strivings of Nature after an unapproachable Ideal, who or which may be unconscious of it. Through PROCLUS, this notion that all orders gaze upwards, and not down on their suffering inferiors, enters Western thought with DIONYSIUS AREOPAGITA and ERIGENA. PLOTINUS clearly expresses a widely current opinion, Enn. v. 2, 1 : ὃν γὰρ τέλειον τῷ μηδὲν ζητεῖν μηδὲ ἔχειν μηδὲ δεῖσθαι, οἷον ὑπερερρύη καὶ τὸ ὑπερπλῆρες Αὐτοῦ πεποίηκεν ἄλλο· τὸ δὲ γενόμενον εἰς Αὐτὸ ἐπεστράφη καὶ ἐπληρώθη καὶ ἐγένετο πρὸς Αὐτὸ βλέπον καὶ Νοῦς οὕτως. The Higher Powers do not indeed perceive that virtue is gone out of them. they are unaware of what is after all a degeneration or an abortion (ὑστέρημα, ἔκτρωμα). Plato, I believe, stands alone in anticipating the Christian view (though, no doubt, imperfectly), that the world took its rise, not in a fluent passivity from an Original Source, but from the desire of the Creator to communicate His own goodness and happiness to other beings. 'How came it to be so?' asks Lotze (*Philos. of Rel.* xlvi). 'Is this transition to Reality an Emanation by natural necessity from God's Being? or is it the act of a Will which gave reality to that which understanding and imagination could only represent as possible? . . . .' (xlviii) : 'If the Divine Thought of the World is to have a realization other than that which it already has in the Divine Mind, this can only be by God's creating *individual finite Spirits*, by His causing to arise in them the cosmic thoughts in question as external perceptions . . . . and at this rate Creation may be defined as follows; God permitted the thought, which at first was only His, to become the thought of other Spirits.' . . . . (li) : 'We cannot wish to define the exact way in which Creation issued forth from the Creator, but only the import of the creative act, which is this: that with a view to the existence of the Spirit-World, *which of itself is no natural consequence flowing from the being of God, a Divine Will* was necessary . . . . And this is how the notion of *Creation* differs from that of an *Emanation* or development of this world.' . . . . (lii) : 'Religious feeling has ever regarded as God's motive (in creating the world) the expansive love, which urges Him to communicate His holiness to other beings, and this thought quite satisfies the yearning in us, which led us to suppose that God *laboured* in creating the world; for according to it, the Creation arose not without this sympathy and enduring interest. It was not a matter-of-fact result flowing from the Divine Will, nor was that Will indifferent; rather is it true that God is bound up with Creation by a perpetual sympathy.' ('Αγαθὸς ἦν, ἀγαθῷ δὲ οὐδεὶς περὶ οὐδενὸς οὐδέποτε ἐγγίγνεται φθόνος· τούτου δ' ἐκτὸς ὢν πάντα ὅτι μάλιστα γένεσθαι ἐβουλήθη παραπλήσια ἑαυτῷ.) A recent commentator on this passage warns us: 'Of course Plato's words are not to be interpreted with a crude literalness.' (!) What is the *Symbolic* or allegoric meaning of goodness? is a question which may arise in some minds. φθόνος is the characteristic feature of mythologic deities; indifference (the mean) of later philosophic substitutes; benevolence (conscious and determinate) at the root of things is a conception found but rarely: modern speculation has laboriously revived the antique belief in Jealousy or Indifference.

Creator of this world in his condemnation of its faults or inequalities, and professes to rise above this sphere to a Deity of unknown inexpressible transcendence, by the simple process of laying aside all the properties and attributes of man (and often all the virtues and decencies as well). It need hardly be pointed out that all these various views extend in the same direction; and are aimed against the humanity of the Divine. Whether the school starts from an admiration or from an abhorrence of the process of life, each will end in a final doctrine not dissimilar to Brâhmanism. In a word, the common object of all speculators in this epoch is to deny Creation, and to deny Providence; and if some seem to welcome the Christian dogma of Redemption and Reconciliation, this is only another term for the announcement of this denial. They worship not that which is, but that which is not [1].

§ 2. But the Christian religion restates the affinity of God with man, and is not ashamed to dwell almost exclusively on the anthropomorphic conception. The history of Christ brings home to us in a startling manner, a truth which was peculiarly unacceptable to the world just then; the supreme interest of God in His handiwork, and His sympathy with His creatures. To an age, which reverenced God just because of His distance and unapproachable majesty, it proclaims that He is very near, and that His providence is very minute. St. Paul may be said to correct the hyper-refinement of Athenian agnosticism by a return to the instinctive sense of affinity with God, in Aratus τοῦ γὰρ καὶ γένος ἐσμεν. Yet the Christian idea of sonship differs entirely from the Stoic *conception*, though not from the *language* of that school. When men, disquieted at the failure of political and social life, believed that the human race is of no more account than birds or insects, a new assurance of dignity, a new guarantee

---

[1] In the account of the Basilidian system depicted by HIPPOLYTUS, it is boldly said that all things yearn after the God who is not. *Ref. Haer.* VII. 22 : Ἐκείνου γάρ, δι' ὑπερβολὴν κάλλους . . . πᾶσα φύσις ὀρέγεται.

of worth was given, which enabled each man to look upon his own personality, however to all seeming valueless, as, in a sense, the supreme end of all creation, nay, the cause of the historic sufferings of Godhead (ὑπὲρ οὗ Χριστὸς ἀπέθανεν).

The preaching of the Gospel revives in a very striking way, the sense of personal dignity in man, and builds on this its ethical system (not as some superficially suppose, upon an appeal to altruism in the first place). God really created the world, and did so for a moral purpose. The visible universe is not the mere shadow, the inseparable correlate of His spiritual and unseen nature; but has been built, a temporary edifice to serve an eternal design.

Man (man the individual, not the race) becomes again the centre of the Universe, and is not a bubble blown about for a season by the winds of Chance or Fate, but possesses an intrinsic verity and the germ of an immortal existence. So far from being an accident in the great total of the Universe, a ripple on a troubled ocean soon to return thither indistinguishable whence it came forth, the Individual is the only reality; so far from being the puppet of an irresistible and unconscious power, his free will is the single ultimate fact of experience, his good will the one thing of final value. His welfare so far from being subordinate to any vague design of arbitrary power or desire for life, is sacrificed to nothing, but is the final end at which Creation aims. The pagan lost sight of the single life in admiration of the Macrocosm; and the sole remaining ethical duty or road to happiness was the loss of the fatal and perhaps impious dower of personality. The unit for the Jew was the Hebrew nation; and he appropriated to himself its failures and successes with the same earnest yet immature self-devotion that we find in Codrus or Decius. But the Christian saw in the world's course, a school for the discipline of character, the apprenticeship of the infant 'that was learning to become a citizen of heaven'[1]. It would not be hard in theory to attack the Christian system as an inculcation of debasing selfishness, were not this accusation immediately contradicted by actual experience. For in this way only (such is the verdict gained by an unbiassed scrutiny of the several schools of *pagan* Individualism) does the value and use of this life appear, if it be not considered as an *accidental* or a *final* good, but as a means to an eternal end. The duties of social life, and genuine interest in others are only possible to those who see in the State (or even in the Church), not an organism whose corporate welfare or exterior prosperity is the final norm of good and bad, but a home of souls; and who discern, through the inequalities of faculty, talent, station, the brotherhood of man. The mists of Platonism which raises qualities and ideas to divine honours, and depreciates the singular, pass away in this more practical view of life. Such a religion is not only readily intelligible to the humblest capacity; but by it alone is the gifted speculator saved from despair at the meaningless futility of his own life, from contempt of the pettiness of others. For it cannot be deemed a satisfactory answer to the riddle of existence to discover that there is none.

§ 3. The Gospel of Christ is a vindication of the personal to the personal. It professes, as no other system does, to justify the world-process, the design of a creator, the dealings of Providence, to the individual consciousness. All other schemes, all other religions are at the mercy of a revolt of Egoism, and this is both natural and inevitable. (This is clear from the practical result of a perversion of Christianity itself, which emphasizing the divine attributes of omnipotence

---

[1] DIO CHRYSOSTOMUS, *Borysthenitica*, Oration 36 :-- The world we must call μίαν . . . . εὐδαίμονα πολιτείαν, ... τὴν θεῶν πρὸς ἀλλήλους κοινωνίαν, and if one shall include σύμπαν τὸ Λογικόν, men being numbered with gods, ὡς παῖδες σὺν ἀνδράσι λέγονται μετέχειν πόλεως, φύσει πολῖται ὄντες, οὐ τῷ φρονεῖν τε καὶ πράττειν τὰ τῶν πολιτῶν οὐδὲ τῷ κοινωνεῖν τοῦ νόμου, ἀσύνετοι ἔτι ὄντες αὐτοῦ.

and will to the exclusion of Love, refuses to justify its doctrine either to the individual reason or the moral sense. The only answer to every natural question put by instinct of justice or self-love, is with TERTULLIAN, '*quia Deus voluit.*' But the matter ends there: not only for children to whom a parent's command should be sufficient, but for grown men, who need an explanation, i.e. demand that a given edict should be justified to themselves. For the only explanation which satisfies is a reference to a personal will, making for a good and beneficent end. We cannot wonder then at J. S. Mill's remarks upon such a conception of deity, nor at the bitter attack at the French Revolution on the tyrannical and arbitrary rather than the paternal view, which not only does not console or encourage the individual, but irritates his natural and indeed commendable selfishness, by ignoring his welfare. This rebellion of Egoism whatever its final conclusion, is a sign of maturity. The youth is of age, and fancies he must claim admittance to his father's councils and secrets. It takes form first as a Sophistic disbelief in social convention and antique institutions, which appear to press heavily on the liberty of the more spirited and ingenious, or it may be represented as in the first book of the Bible, as the passing of adult reason out of the Paradise of children; where an apparently arbitrary command or restriction is first questioned and then transgressed [1]. The certainty of our own

---

[1] SCHELLING'S earliest work in Latin, an attempt to explain 'the very ancient philosopheme in Genesis iii, *de primâ Malorum hum. origine*,' is worth consulting § 5. 'It is wrong to suppose as hitherto, mali moralis initia hoc capite describi. It is rather the decay of the Golden Age, a passing forth from primitive simplicity, the dawn of reason and intelligence, from which at once arise the conquests and the pains of civilized life. The cause of this "evil" is supposed by all to have been curiosity; this well agrees with Pandora's legend among the Greeks. The gates of a childish Paradise are closed for ever on the human race; they wander forth in search of the Ideal (rerum altiorum cupiditas), and their pioneer is the Snake, an inner spirit of discontent, which is cause of all unhappiness and of all advance.' § 6. 'It is Reason, driving us by main force out of the narrow realm of sense, promising us a home which we never reach, glories that we are never to behold!

Subordinate Dualism. 141

existence is our most vivid experience in practical life; and those who after the advice of Seneca to Lucilius, 'alternate solitude with Society' and thus are neither immersed in the State nor completely anchoritic,—are brought to a conclusion that may seem vain and indemonstrable, but is inevitable: that the world is formed to produce self-consciousness; that it cannot be the design (if at this stage such a term is admissible)—the design of the world-process to extinguish a result so painfully attained; that in spite of all appearance the education and discipline of the personal spirit is the aim of creation; and that the author of this system, while He transcends all human excellence, yet bears resemblance to men in two essential points; He must be supreme *goodness* and Love; and He must be supreme *justice*. He must be known as *Creator* of the world, and *Judge* of mankind; indifferent neither to their *happiness* nor their *virtue*: and these in the end are identical.

The Platonist or Gnostic of this period considers all such direct interference with phenomena derogatory to the highest God[1]. Behind the duality of the Powers in their *natural* and

---

In future, there is no hope of a return to the unreasoning state of happy innocence in Eden or Arcadia.' 'Who would prefer' (he asks, in a burst of enthusiasm, significant enough in 1792) 'the sty to such a glorious and infinite destiny?' Compare also the Lactantian interpolator, D. I vii 5.

[1] PSEUDO-PLUTARCH, *Plac. Philos.* I. 6. PLATO's creationism is rebuked (ὄζει λήρου Βεκκεσελήνου); κοινῶς οὖν ἁμαρτάνουσιν ἀμφότεροι (Plato and Anaxagoras) ὅτι τὸν Θεὸν ἐποίησαν ἐπιστρεφόμενον τῶν ἀνθρωπίνων ἢ καὶ τούτου χάριν τὸν κόσμον κατασκευάζοντα Τὸ γὰρ μακάριον καὶ ἄφθαρτον ζῶον, συμπεπληρωμένον τε πᾶσι τοῖς ἀγαθοῖς καὶ κακοῦ παντὸς ἄδεκτον, ὅλον ὂν περὶ τὴν συνοχὴν τῆς ἰδίας εὐδαιμονίας καὶ ἀφθαρσίας ἀνεπίστρεφές ἐστι τῶν ἀνθρωπίνων πραγμάτων. Κακοδαίμων δ' ἂν εἴη, ἐργάτου δίκην καὶ τέκτονος, ἀχθοφορῶν καὶ μεριμνῶν εἰς τὴν τοῦ κόσμου κατασκευήν.

So much for the *physical* development of the world, where the influence of the Highest Deity appeared unimaginable: it was the same in the *historical*; —πῶς δὲ εἴπερ ὁ Θεὸς ἔστι, καὶ τῇ τούτου φροντίδι τὰ κατ' ἄνθρωπον οἰκονομεῖται, τὸ μὲν κίβδηλον εὐτυχεῖ. τὸ δ' ἀστεῖον τἀναντία πάσχει; CELSUS does indeed believe in Providence, but it is administered through inferior agents: Condescension of the Supreme Being to man he could not understand. It was an axiom of philosophic religion that all direct communication, *except dimly in*

historical activity, there stands the Philonian λόγος; and even this power is too much qualified and bears too many attributes to be regarded as the ultimate principle; and a *neuter* word, which expresses not so much the conscious *Source* as the indefinite *Ground* of existence, has to be introduced. The later Platonic theology is a continual straining after something still more abstract and completely negative and one, as if determined to put an end to the anthropomorphic superstition of the divine image in Man; and to separate finally the Author from his work, not perhaps by the primitive dualism of the master of the School, but by an ever-increasing series of intermediate beings or stages, which perplexed and discouraged the aspirant to reunion with the only true life. But the

thought (ORIGEN, *c Celsum*, vii. 40, 42) was impossible. ' Man is not formed in God's image (vi. 63-4), nor is he any dearer to God than animals; indeed, many tribes have a far closer affinity (ἐγγυτέρω τῆς θείας ὁμιλίας ἐκεῖνα πεφυκέναι, καὶ εἶναι σοφώτερα καὶ θεοφιλέστερα, iv. 88). It is an absurd superstition to believe that the world was made for us men (iv. 69, 23), or that the highest truth is entrusted to a single nation, or the simplicity of ignorant faith; or, indeed, that there is any absolute and universal religious truth at all.'

The distance between God and the world (which can only be called *His* by a stretch of imagination) he expresses as follows :—Λέγω δὲ οὐδὲν καινόν, ἀλλὰ παλαι δεδογμένα. Ὁ Θεὸς ἀγαθός ἐστι, καὶ καλὸς καὶ εὐδαίμων, καὶ ἐν τῷ καλλίστῳ καὶ ἀρίστῳ. Εἰ δὴ ἐς ἀνθρώπους κάτεισι, μεταβολῆς αὐτῷ δεῖ· μεταβολῆς δὲ ἐξ ἀγαθοῦ εἰς κακόν . . . . καὶ ἐξ εὐδαιμονίας εἰς κακοδαιμονίαν. Τίς ἂν οὖν ἕλοιτο τοιαύτην μεταβολήν; . . . . οὐκ ἂν οὖν οὐδὲ ταύτην τὴν μεταβολὴν Θεὸς δέχοιτο (iv. 14). By which easy syllogistic method the speculators of the late Hellenic and Imperial age unanswerably refuted the beliefs in Direct Creation, Providence, Revelation; and sent the religious minds to find what solace could be afforded for this neglect, to the mysteries of Isis and Mithra, and the worship of particular and local Daemons. Such a theory tended to support the Roman system, for the Emperor, like the Supreme Deity, was unquestionable and inscrutable, and the pettiness of civic worship (to which CELSUS, no less than LUCIAN and SEXTUS EMPIRICUS, recalled men) prevented any serious coalition in a universal Faith.—Οὔκουν ἀνθρώπῳ πεποίηται τὰ πάντα, ὥσπερ οὐδὲ λέοντι, οὐδ' ἀέτῳ, οὐδὲ δελφῖνι· ἀλλ' ὅπως ὅδε ὁ Κόσμος ὡς ἂν θεοῦ ἔργον . . . . τέλειον ἐξ ἁπάντων γένηται. Τούτου χάριν μεμέτρηται τὰ πάντα, οὐκ ἀλλήλων, εἰ μὴ πάρεργον, ἀλλὰ τοῦ Ὅλου· καὶ μέλει τῷ Θεῷ τοῦ ὅλου, καὶ τοῦτο οὔποτε ἀπολείπει Πρόνοια . . . . οὐδὲ διὰ χρόνου πρὸς αὐτὸν (?) ὁ Θεὸς ἐπιστρέφει, οὐδ' ἀνθρώπων ἕνεκα ὀργίζεται (IV. 99). If the Stoics, with EPICTETUS and AURELIUS, have become Platonic in this age, the Platonists have borrowed the Stoic doctrine of a *universal*, not a *particular* Providence.

Christian insists upon this double office of good *Creator* and moral *Judge*, not as the deputed province of some inferior power, but as the essential and inseparable function of the Highest God Himself. 'The Shadow of the Sage's self, projected on vacancy,' was called God; and the Sage had long abandoned interest in the practical life, and expected his Divinity to do the same. But the Christian sees in God a father, and a redeemer, believes in a minute providence never wearied by trifles so called, but overruling all for the best; not some distant being, who takes delight in the Universe as an eternal spectacle, but a consoler ever near to the worshipper, piercing through the outer surroundings to the good-will and honouring and rewarding it alone. Everything else has been stripped off; there is no longer any vain groping amid unrealities, no fruitless pursuit of the object outside all reference to ourselves; but the true life of the world is seen to consist of one relation only, a personal God in immediate contact with personal man.

§ 4. Some such preface on the novelty of the Christian message is required, to throw light on the problem of Evil and its interpretation just at that time. It will be seen that owing to this shifting of the centre of gravity from the Universe to man, an entirely new conception of sin, pain, and evil generally must arise. There is no *end* in creation acknowledged now outside and beyond the perfection of human character; everything must take its place in some subordinate relation to this final aim. This by no means simplifies matters; and the main doctrine of the *personal interest of God in the world*, increases the difficulties which surround the origin and purpose of evil. In that view of the world, (which in future I shall describe for the sake of brevity as the *Impersonal* conception)—the question πόθεν τὰ κακά; is not unanswerable and can be easily eluded by a subtle dialectician. The curiosity of an inquirer who is not yet fully self-conscious, or who has discovered the secret treasure of his personality only to lose it, may be without difficulty disarmed.

Such pantheistic systems, which make the present and the actual (as a meaningless and infinite series of phenomena), both eternal and divine, must needs eliminate all notion of *purpose* or of *progress*. There can be no history in such a universe. 'Here and now, Deity is perfectly revealed in its two aspects, as thought or as extension.' The inventors of such systems have abandoned all hopes of explanation: they will merely codify existing things, and invent a formula that may satisfy the intellect; and afterwards with more or less poetic sentiment pronounce the result beautiful or detestable, and style the whole, *best* or *worst* of all possible worlds. 'Heaven and earth shall pass away, but my words shall not pass away'; the doctrine of the eternity of the universe was seen to be incompatible with Christianity[1]. Nor can the optimist quarrel with the pessimist for imposing his own final construction on

---

[1] Compare the anti-Platonic writings of AENEAS of GAZA, and ZACHARIAS of MITYLENE. NEMESIUS had for an instant endeavoured to reconcile with Christian faith the two cardinal doctrines of Neo-Platonism, the pre existence of souls, the eternity of the world; both fatal to the supreme dignity of the Personal.—AENEAS and ZACHARIAS set themselves to disprove them (p. 52, ed. Boissonade) *Theophrastus*: Οἱ τοῦ Πλάτωνος μυσταγωγοὶ τὸ γέγονεν οὐ γέγονε λέγουσιν, ἀλλὰ κατ' αἰτίαν ἐγένετο, οἷον τῆς ἐμῆς σκιᾶς αἴτιον τοὐμὸν σῶμα· ἀλλ' οὐκ αὐτὸ πεποίηκεν αὐτήν, ἀλλ' ἐκείνη τούτῳ συνηκολούθησεν. To which *Euxitheus* replies. Οὐκ ἄρα δημιουργὸς ὁ Δημιουργὸς εἰ μὴ βουλόμενος ὃ πεποίηκε δημιουργεῖ, ἀλλ' αὐτόματον τόδε τὸ Πᾶν, εἰ μὴ γέγονεν. . . . . Οὐκοῦν καὶ τὴν Πρόνοιαν ὁ τῶν ἀνοήτων λόγος συνανεῖλεν· οὐ γὰρ ἂν γένοιτο σκιᾶς ἐπιμέλεια—ZACHARIAS, 105, Boiss.: Φασὶ γὰρ ὅτι, καθάπερ αἴτιον τὸ σῶμα τῆς ἑκάστου σκιᾶς γίνεται, ὁμόχρονος δὲ τῷ σώματι ἡ σκιὰ καὶ οὐχ ὁμότιμος οὕτω δὴ καὶ ὅδε ὁ Κόσμος παρακολούθημά ἐστι τοῦ Θεοῦ, αἰτίου ὄντος αὐτῷ τοῦ εἶναι, καὶ συναΐδιός ἐστι τῷ Θεῷ οὐκέτι δὲ καὶ ὁμότιμος.—115, Boiss.: Εἰ δ' ἀγαθὸς ἂν ἐβουλήθη εἶναι τὰ ὄντα, οὐ δεόμενος αὐτῶν πρὸς τὸ εἶναι (ἦν γὰρ πρὸ τούτων ὡς τελειότατος καὶ οὐδενὸς δεόμενος, αὐτὸς ὢν ἡ πᾶσα αὐτάρκεια), οὐκ ἄρα ἀνάγκη συναΐδιον εἶναι τῷ πεποιηκότι τὸ ποίημα· δεῖ γὰρ πρεσβύτερον εἶναι τοῦ ποιήματος τὸν ποιητήν . . . . εἴπερ τὸ ποιούμενον δεύτερόν ἐστι τοῦ ποιοῦντος αἰτίᾳ καὶ χρόνῳ, εἰ μέλλει μὴ ἀβούλητος αἰτία τυγχάνειν καὶ οὐ λελογισμένη (ὥσπερ τῆς σκιᾶς τὸ σῶμα) . . . . Πῶς γὰρ ἂν εἴη δημιουργὸς ὁ Δημιουργὸς εἰ μὴ βουλόμενος ὃ πεποίηκεν εἴη δημιουργός; ἢ εἰ ὥσπερ τῷ σώματι ἡ σκιὰ οὕτως ἁπλῶς καὶ τῷ Δημιουργῷ παρηκολούθησεν ἐκ ταὐτομάτου παρυποστὰν τόδε τὸ Πᾶν;

the ambiguous results of the scrutiny of things. Both are indeed fully justified; and like all interpretations of this kind each betrays the inmost character of the philosopher; though nominally aiming at *impersonal* truth, each involves an act of moral choice, and proves that the *personal* cannot be silenced[1]: for what is pessimism but the natural reaction of the neglected individual against the eulogies of a Universe, which may be *absolutely* good (whatever possible sense this can have), but is certainly not good in relation to him? In such system then the terms good and bad gradually tend to lose their meaning. They are different manifestations of the same thing; the law of polarity is welcomed by such speculators[2]. In old days, Plato had suggested an explanation by a sort of allegorical hypothesis; God works on a pre-existent matter, and His beneficence is thwarted by the intractable material; or again, original creation is entrusted to inferior deities, and the subsequent care of the world to Daemons. There is no actual and final antithesis of good and evil; no promise of a final triumph of the right, such as might perhaps encourage the Parsee of ancient days; a question perhaps of *stages*, of higher and lower, but not of absolute contraries. The two terms shade off insensibly into each other. There is no clear boundary line of demarcation.

In any case Evil (regarded only in relation to abstractions, to the unconscious, not to the individual who painfully experiences it), tends to disappear, to be considered as non-existent. And this is true, whatever be the precise form of Pantheism in favour.

§ 5. Christianity supplants this *physical* conception of evil by a *moral* explanation. It does not reside as a property in matter, for in its very nature it is inapplicable to anything that is not conscious and free. It can only be understood in

---

[1] See the very remarkable words of ROMANES, *Thoughts on Religion*, 101-2, 112, 135.
[2] Compare SAMUEL LAING, *A Modern Zoroastrian*.

a *personal* sense. The world no longer flows out from the overfull and brimming cup of God's nature (τὸ ὑπερπλῆρες in PLOTINUS); it is created by Him for a certain and very definite purpose. Evil and matter (so often involved or identified) are no longer the shadow cast by the divine perfection; but the one is His handiwork (and as such *good*, but not *god*); the other is a criminal and deliberate rebellion of a perverse will against His decrees, which are not arbitrary but loving. And on the other side, the ideal set before us is neither the superficial welfare of a nation, nor the progress of civilized humanity, nor even the outward glory of a church, but the education of single souls. As there is nothing that can be called good unreservedly but a 'good will,' so it is impossible to connect the notion of intrinsic Evil with anything but an Evil Will, a person [1].

[1] The methodical Pantheist, who upholds the omnipotence of God at the expense of all other Divine qualities, in vain repeats the unmeaning paradox 'that vice is not less hateful or less deserving of punishment because it is involuntary.' MANILIUS, who as a poet marks the transition of pure Stoic Positivism into a mystic region, and is in a sense the counterpart of Cicero, labours to show the hatefulness of fated evil, and the responsibility of automata: iv. 112:—

'Nam neque mortiferas quisquam magis ederit herbas
Quod non *arbitrio* veniunt, sed *semine certo*;
Gratia nec levior tribuetur dulcibus escis,
Quod *Natura* dedit fruges, non ulla *voluntas*:—
Sic hominum meritis tanto sit gloria maior
Quod caelo gaudente venit; rursusque nocentes
Oderimus magis, in culpam poenasque creatos
(= σκεύη κατηρτισμένα εἰς ἀπώλειαν)
Nec refert scelus unde cadat, scelus esse fatendum.

Jonathan Edwards (*Doctrine of Original Sin*, 1758, Boston) is reduced to unintelligible refinement to avoid a logical conclusion:—' The Divine Being is not the author of Sin, but only disposes things in such a manner that Sin will certainly ensue.' No doubt we are right in applying the title Almighty to the Creator, but an exclusive study of this quality of Omnipotence leads us back insensibly to the old discarded *physical* conception of the Divine nature. The highest wonder in the Universe is not the *Power* of God, but His free gift of personality and independence to reasonable creatures. Edwards, too, echoes the Doctrine of MANILIUS in the following opinion:—' The essence of Virtue and Vice, as they exist in the disposition of the Heart, and are manifested in the acts of the Will, lies not in their *cause* but in their *Nature*' (*Freedom of*

Other so-called evils are only *apparent* or *relative* Evils, or blessings in disguise [1]; other imperfections or errors may be due to ignorance or incomplete knowledge—all such belong to time, and are curable; but a fully-conscious and deliberately perverse will must be regarded as eternal in the sense of rejecting its own remedy; for God (this is a valuable lesson which Plato taught) acts on the soul as on the world, not by *compulsion*, but by *persuasion*.

This may perhaps explain how it is that to the Personalist, the idea of an Evil Spirit, who in a sense *thwarts* and in another *fulfils* the designs of Providence is by no means an obsolete superstition, but a doctrine of the highest truth and importance.

§ 6. A second point remains to be considered; in what does personality consist? It is discovered to be the final and unalterable fact of experience [2] (for even Natural Science does not discover things in themselves, but only expresses

---

the Will, Boston, 1754). 'The possession of the sinful disposition by which men are unable to obey the commands of God is itself their worst and most inexcusable sin' (Letter to Mr. Erskine).

Yet it must not be supposed that Edwards maintained throughout the same implacable resentment against the just claims of the personal. In a posthumous work (*God's Last End in Creation*, Boston, 1788), he contends rightly enough ' that there is no incompatibility between the *happiness* of created beings and the declarative glory of God, inasmuch as these two ends coincide in one. The Creation as happy and holy, as it is the object of the benevolent love of the Creator, cannot but declare His glory.' In a similar manner, the seeming austerity of Kant's *Law of Duty* is softened by a firm conviction or, rather, fervent hope and trust, that Virtue and Happiness are in their nature inseparable, or at least will in the end coincide. 'We are bound to seek to further that harmony between Virtue which is the Highest Good (*Supremum Bonum*) and Happiness, which is the indispensable condition of the realization of Perfect Good (S. Bonum in the sense of *Bonum* Consummatum).' Nay, on this he founds the chief reason for the existence of God; ' we must postulate the existence of a cause, which shall be able to effect the exact degree of agreement of Happiness with Morality; = we must postulate the existence of God.'

[1] We may here fully endorse the language of CELSUS, who tersely sums up the conclusions of Stoic and Platonic thought (in this age hardly distinguishable currents): iv. 70: Κἄν σοί τι δοκῇ κακόν, οὔπω δῆλον εἰ κακόν ἐστιν· οὐ γὰρ οἶσθ' ὅ τι ἢ σοι ἢ ἄλλῳ ἢ τῷ Ὅλῳ συμφέρει.

[2] Compare ROMANES, l. c. 130, § 10.

their relations to us, in terms of ourselves). But what is its nature? The essence of Personality rightly conceived is self-limitation. *Creation is the voluntary limitation which God has imposed on Himself.* And creation in this new view (which refuses to work up to self-consciousness, but insists on beginning from it) can only be regarded as a creation of free spirits[1]. Any other conception of the act is more or less inconceivable. We cannot escape from ourselves; and from a sense of responsible worth. The notion of free-will may be 'an inevitable illusion,' but the emphasis is on the first word of the definition, and an illusion is often truer for us than truth itself[2]. Regarding then man, one by one rather than in the aggregate, as the final end of creation (and in a sense perhaps the beginning also), we must hold to our belief in spite of the taunts levelled at our mistaken notion of our value[3]. Now since the Personalist must regard creation as a deliberate and moral act (not as a necessary outflowing of unconscious perfection), *it is clear that omnipotence, in the usual sense of the word, can no longer form one of the primary attributes of the Divine Nature.* It is a truer form of almighty power to submit to limitation; and this the Christian believes to be the main doctrine of his faith. God limits Himself in time, He sacrifices Himself in submitting to the bonds of matter; not as if this self-emptying were an eternal process, but as a means to some great and benevolent end; the communication of His own nature to free beings. God, if I may reverently use the expression, submits, not indeed to a development, but to a circumscription, in history. He pleads with man, and while He seems to educate the race, is acting for the sake of the single life. The Son of God to complete our redemption, does not

---

[1] Compare Lotze's *Outlines of the Philosophy of Religion.*
[2] Lord Kames opined that 'God had deceived mankind by an invincible instinct or feeling, which leads them to suppose that they are free.'
[3] Compare Leopardi's *Dialogue ' of the Goblin and the Gnome.'*

shrink from suffering and death, that henceforward a man may say, not only 'Our Father,' but 'My Saviour.'

In sum, the visible world in Christianity is not the expression of God, but His self-limitation (in a sense also, His disguise); and the course of history represents the rejection of the Almighty, and the sufferings of the Lord of Glory.

PART II.

GOD (CREATOR AND JUDGE) AND THE ORIGIN OF EVIL.

§ 1. Nothing need now detain us from the promised consideration of two remarkable writers in the Ante-Nicene period, the author of the Pseudo-CLEMENTINE literature[1], and LACTANTIUS[2]. We have seen the tendency of orthodox

---

[1] The CLEMENTINE literature: works written probably in Syria towards the middle or close of the second century, and claiming CLEMENT of Rome for their author: earliest form no doubt the most violent, polemical, and doctrinal (Ebionitic); owing to the interest of the narrative (in which CLEMENT starts from Rome to hear Christ, falls in with Peter, and at last discovers his parent, after witnessing all Peter's conflicts with Simon Magus), these writings secured the sympathy of the orthodox, and the *Homilies* were corrected and altered, so as to remove points of difference, and concentrate attention on the romance and its incidents. *The Recognitions* is the name given to RUFFINUS's translation of the original work, in which he boldly exercises his well-known power of excision and modification. The stages of this process of adaptation to orthodox readers very possibly were: (1) the early and now lost *Archetype*, where doctrinal hostility had the chief place; (2) *Homilies*, which we have in Greek, in which story and polemic have an equal share; (3) RUFFINUS's translation, or the *Recognitions*, where dogma is becoming subordinate; (4) the *Epitome*, where the story as such monopolizes all attention, and the sermons and debates have fallen out. The general teaching of the Clementines will be seen from the quotations which follow.

[2] L. CAELIUS FIRMIANUS (circ. 260-340 A.D), a contemporary of the Neo-Platonist Iamblichus; a pupil of ARNOBIUS the Numidian, but not an imitator of his style; professed rhetoric at Nicomedia between the years 305-312 A.D. (*Div. Inst.* v. 2); 'in extreme old age,' as Jerome tells us, was the tutor of Crispus, the son of Constantine I, in Gaul, 319 A.D. He wrote (1) seven books of *Divine Instructions*, on the model of his master's work, in which he contrasts the true religion with vain superstition on the one hand, and proud philosophy on the other; (2) *De Opificio Dei*, to Demetrianus;

Christianity to emphasize the personal element in GOD (that is, His self-limitation), and the personal element in man, his accountability, and therefore his freedom. The one hypothesis seems to explain the title *Creator*, the second the function of *Judge*, both of which meet us at every turn in the Anti-Gnostical writings. There is thus both *purpose* and *progress* in the world: and the definite goal to which creation moves is the judgement of man, rational and responsible. It is never pretended that this conception of the world explains the existence of evil adequately; the believer can only say, 'Free-will, with which we start as a postulate, is inconceivable without the possibility of lapse; and the results of perseverance in a particular course may become a permanent and ineffaceable habit. God might have created blameless puppets, but while we are constituted as we are, it is impossible to sincerely attach to such creatures a notion of merit; just as it is impossible with justice to punish ignorance save with a view to its correction. God might indeed have foreseen and prevented the fall of angels and men; but as He has, though foreseeing, not prevented, we can only suppose that in a mysterious manner evil, which apparently baffles the purpose of God in the world, is made (in a still more comprehensive monistic doctrine) to serve His eternal end; the probation, redemption, and eternal happiness of Free Spirits.'

It is at this point precisely that we are met by the greatest obstacle. Is the evil spirit *independent* then of God, or is he still His *servant*? a *rival*, or a *minister*? There can be no doubt that these two notions coincide in the Christian

---

(3) the *Epitome* of the *Div. Instit.* to Pentadius; (4) *On the Anger of God*, against the Epicureans, to Donatus; (5) the work *On the Death of Persecutors* may or may not be his (it is headed 'Lucius Caecilius,' and dedicated to Donatus): an interesting historical account in accurate style of the fate of persecuting emperors, especially at the beginning of the fourth century. His Latinity has been all the more admired since his orthodoxy has been impeached. JEROME, *Ep.* 58: 'Utinam tam nostra affirmare potuisset, quam facile aliena destruxit!'

doctrine of the Devil, which, as contrasted with Gnostic or Manichaean speculation, never attributes to him original coexistence with God, but a *created* life in time; yet sometimes seems to convey the idea of successful opposition to divine counsels. One object of the PSEUDO-CLEMENTINES is without doubt to investigate the nature of Evil, and its place in a universe which was created by a moral Being, just and merciful, and which cannot be regarded as the abortion of an inferior divinity. We find in them a crude yet working hypothesis to account for this; and there is a distinct point of contact with LACTANTIUS in the dogma of Syzygies (ὁ κανὼν τῆς Συζυγίας). The first impulse of the writer of the *Homilies*, which I take to be the earlier unmodified form, is to refute a certain form of Gnôsis, and to point to the true remedy for such heresies, in a resolute excision of scriptural interpolations, which arise from a perverted Judaism. This religion (whose historical fortress the various forces of Gnosticism beleaguered) must be restated as a *spiritual*, not a *ceremonious* faith. In fact, one form of Gnôsis is employed to combat another: a modified Marcionitism is to correct, without breaking from, the Old Testament; and the writer aims at discovering the original primitive religion, identical in the true Jew and the true Christian, and now for the first time thrown open to the whole Gentile world. There is a certain honesty in this method of dealing with inconvenient Scripture; allegory is not tolerated in this severe school: 'ense recidendum est, ne pars sincera trahatur.' What is unworthy of God is interpolated; and the power of discriminating genuine from false has come with the advent of the True Prophet. 'But how is it that God's word has been allowed to suffer this violation?' The answer is significant of the whole mental attitude of the writer; 'to *test* the perspicacity of the reader, and prove if a *natural instinct* of what is right and wrong, suitable and in-apt for the Divine Being, could escape slavery to a written letter'; in a word, to encourage personal inquiry, led indeed by a sense of right (τὸ εὔλογον), and to dignify beyond an inspired book the free and innate knowledge of God, which every man possesses.

§ 2. The God revealed by this eternal religion is before all things personal, Creator, Governor, Judge. There is no original antithesis of co-ordinate principles; nor any scheme of higher and lower spheres which ends in pagan Gnosticism by dissociating the idea of Creation and Providence from the Supreme God. The world is built for man's sake; and, for his further discipline, for his education into self-knowledge and self-reliance, a duality of influences, evil and good, are called into play, from Cain and Abel down to Simon Magus and Peter, culminating in the final appearance of Antichrist and Christ. The evil in the world is explained partly as the will of the Supreme, partly as the necessary probation of man. Sometimes, with a certain inconsistency it is stated that ἡ Κακία (personified evil) sends out her apostles, and again Greek παιδεία all comes from ὁ Κακὸς Δαίμων, while references to evil angels are not uncommon. The True Prophet, who in each emission of pairs appears in the *second* place, is God's spirit, again and again in successive incarnations entering a rebellious world, clothing itself in human flesh, or united to some good man, and on each occasion teaching the same truth: namely, the doctrine of God, *Creator* and *Judge*, the sum, as it were, of Natural Religion, or Exoteric Christianity, in IRENAEUS and ORIGEN;—a stern yet necessary doctrine in an age when the idea of God evaporated in a vague conception of an impassive Benevolence at the root of things, and the freedom and responsibility of man in a determinist 'physical advantage' (φύσεως προτέρημα) of a small minority selected by a non-moral choice. These several Theophanies calling man to true knowledge, and to the hope of a future life, are invariably thwarted, and indeed anticipated, by a corresponding emanation of evil. Such is the main outline of this curious attempt at speculative compromise, the union of true Hebraism and Christianity as the proclamation of one God, Creator and Judge; the refutation of non-ethical Gnôsis and ceremonial Judaism by cutting away all inconvenient scriptural testimony; and the explanation of the obvious struggle of good and evil influences in this world by a (somewhat ambiguous) subordination of Evil to the final purpose of God. *Ethical* as the writer tries to be, a dangerous *physical* interpretation is in the last resort placed upon evil; for both good and evil seem to be the manifestations of an indifferent being in polarity, a sort of counterpart to the strange notions of bifurcation in the original unisexual ADAM KADMON. But, though strict logic may at times seem to drive him to this position, it is nevertheless alien to the general tenor of these writings; for, however fantastic this cosmogony may be, the basis of all such theorizing is an honest conviction of a *moral purpose* in the world as far as its Creator's intention is concerned; and of the moral dignity of man, which by free choice can realize, can co-operate in this purpose. We have before us an ingenious attempt to preserve the unity, goodness, transcendence of God, and His impassibility ($ἀπροσπάθεια$), without at the same time giving the world over entirely to the rule of the Devil, or on the other hand explaining away the significance and existence of evil. The author acknowledges evil as the wilful rebellion of a free-will; but believes that it subserves God's intention. He is thus working on the side of orthodoxy as champion of *personality*. What is his object in Books v, vi, vii? To repudiate current paganism, whether *popular* or *esoteric*; to expose the crimes of mythology, or their seductive allegorization. At the mouth of Appion, a hypocritical priest of a religion of Reserve, we have a strange cosmogony from Chaos, in which Ἔρως, a blind struggle of an unconscious life-principle, takes the place of a purposeful Creator. It is just this [modern] principle of the 'strivings of the Will to live' which excites the hostility of the writer. He feels the inconsistency of a material and unconscious substrate of infinite potentiality [1]. He seems to object to the sudden and uncalled-for intrusion of a 'deus ex machina,' ὁ αἰθέριος τεχνιτής, into a universe, which appears (according to this hypothesis) to have grown up very well by itself. At the beginning of things, he is determined to have a *personal* Mind, and thus in these books strikes a blow at Hylozoism (or the belief that the egg is first), that mysterious and inconceivable doctrine, which we can reconcile neither with our experience nor our reason, but which nevertheless is, and always has been, the fundamental creed of the larger part of mankind, though it be sometimes disguised by personal names and *personified* impulse as in mythology, or as in the Aristotelian metaphor of the yearning (ὄρεξις) of matter after form.

§ 3. On this point we can at least be clear: God is a personal will, absolute, and almighty, whose purpose nothing can oppose: He is by no means formless, but ἔχων μορφήν: else ἐν τίνι ἐρείσῃ [2]; He is not infinite space, but rather the heart of the universe. Next, the world is created for man, by the grace and gift of God, himself a free person; and to set before his choice two kingdoms of *transient* and *eternal* good, two spirits (or influences) are produced. Here then is Man placed for probation between two rival chieftains, tried by interpolated Scriptures, wiles of Daemons, and inherited passions and diseases, and, above all, held in fetters of Πλάνη and Συνήθεια, the hateful antagonist of Ἀλήθεια. The True Prophet comes to restore the primitive Monotheism of the patriarchs, handed down from the saintly and unfallen Adam (who is his earliest incarnation); and to revive pure spiritual Hebraism free from fiery sacrifices, and purified by the new watery birth (for on Baptism and its efficacy the writer especially insists). It is a religion of gratitude to the *Creator*,

---

[1] Compare Dr. H. STIRLING, who shows that this is actually Idealism, in his *Secret of Hegel*.

[2] Compare the complaint of the Egyptian monk in SOCRATES.

fear of the *Judge*. This visible world is indeed the *creation* of God, with its present pleasures and allurements; but there is a greater stress on His moral government (PHILO's βασιλικὴ δύναμις), which places us in these enticing surroundings, not that we may enjoy them, but of deliberate choice (a self-limitation) 'may pass through things temporal' to God himself, and our better home. Very significant of 'CLEMENT'S' emphasis on the *personal* is his distinct rejection of a *Magical* theory of *revelation* or *redemption*, in which divine truth or divine life is appropriated by the entire abandonment or annihilation of the human (which yet must be postulated as the centre and agent of the appropriation). Revelation for man thus placed must come from within, the echo in the heart of God's voice without. External means of information may be fraudulent (scriptures and visions). As opposed to the mechanical and arbitrary theory of inspiration in Philo and in the Apologists (in which the Sun of human reason sets before the dark radiance of the divine night can reign[1]), all heavenly secrets or messages are judged by τὸ εὔλογον, the instinctive and moral sense which each man of birthright possesses, that God is *good* and *just*. It is the canon of *rational probability*[2], III. 31, 32. The opposite view may in a measure be regarded as a corollary of that docetic theophany in which Christ passes through the Virgin, ὥσπερ διὰ σωλῆνος. The divine and the human are incompatible, and, save for an instantaneous moment of miracle, mutually exclude each other. There is no real union of God and man; for the conception of both is still *physical*, infinite and finite, and not *moral;* the supposed reconciliation is of two antithetic *natures*, not the harmony of two free and personal *Wills*.

But to 'CLEMENT' the *appropriation* of one personal will by another must be real and not fictitious. Christ speaks clearly;

---

[1] Compare PHILO's Commentary on Gen. xv. 12: *Rer. Div. Her.* 53.

[2] Which to-day would seem to be ousting the old *à priori* arguments against the possibility of a Divine Revelation.

all, even the most ignorant, can understand; for the True Prophet offers Himself to each man, just as each can receive Him. The human side is not merged in the divine; but remains entire, though transformed to co-operate of free choice, and to enjoy the consciousness of working with God. [But whatever merits the writer of the CLEMENTINE *Homilies* may be justly allowed[1], all are rendered valueless by his imperfect Christology. There is no true reconciliation; and in the end, the justice of God becomes unethical, and the appearance of Christ a transient theophany. Yet, as it is not with the doctrine of Christ's Person that I am now concerned, but with the Prince of the Left, the above commendation may be allowed to hold good in this latter relation.]

§ 4. In the doctrine of Evil (founded upon this *moral* view of the person of God and man) an attempt is made to infuse an *ethical* significance into a *physical* and necessitarian conception of the Divine Nature and the world-process. The Supreme Being, possibly in perverted Rabbinism, and certainly in many Gnostic sects, is regarded as bisexual, hermaphroditic; as containing, that is, within Himself, a lower element, destined to issue in a more or less fictitious conflict; ' that in God, which is not yet God,' to borrow an idea which is found in BEHMEN, and lies at the root of much transcendental cosmogony, in the earlier years of this century. Without forsaking this hypothesis (an immediate expression in polarity, by contraries), our writer,—determined opponent of impersonalism, and starting from an assumption of fully-conscious and purposeful reason,—transforms the idea of evil from a necessary development of a certain side in the Divine Nature (inconceivable when so much importance was attached to the *simplicity* of τὸ ὄν) into a deliberate creation, designed for the *moral* discipline of man. With much honesty of purpose, and boldness of enterprise, the writer cannot come to a satisfactory or con-

---

[1] Compare the remarks of Mr. Simon, note YYY. Div. I, vol. i. of DORNER's work, Clark's Translation.

sistent conclusion. For with the best wishes he has not brought out the real *ethical* conception of sin, and there remains in the picture of the world-spirit a *physical* notion which in the end either throws back the entire guilt upon the Creator (so-called *Augustinian*), or, regarding evil as necessary to development and moral choice, denies its essential evilness altogether (*Platonist*).

In the citations it will be seen how the old problem occurs (at last to be dismissed as insoluble),—the problem which we have thus stated: Is the Devil a *rival* or a *servant* of God? The former is the conception most in favour with Personalists, inasmuch as wilful defiance of a good law by a free being is the only intelligible kind of evil. But in the difficulty of this mode of thought, the author takes refuge in a physical notion; the devil was 'created to rejoice at the punishment of the bad,' and to find pleasure in a certain habitation, where such punishment was to be exercised; and in this latter case he is blameless, for his constitution, as agent of a lower province, the divine displeasure and justice, is *naturally* or of *necessity* such as God made him; while on occasion, by an omission which cannot be otherwise described than as shifty and inexcusable, he is spoken of as 'created to rejoice in evil,' and not in its punishment. 'The evil principle' (says DORNER's commentator) 'serves (the Good) without either knowing or willing to do so; for though Satan *himself* is not righteous as God is, his *work* is righteous. When he does mischief, he is executing a divine punishment, which God as the Good cannot *Himself* directly administer.' Accordingly, he is compelled, without being aware of it, 'to help on the victory of the righteous God.' But whatever the strict definition of the Devil's freedom or responsibility for the part he plays, to him as to a supreme world-spirit is entrusted visible creation; he is the lord of the kingdom of transient good things. It is not an usurpation so much as a lawful commission or delegation of authority. He rules over pagan ideas of present enjoyment and brief pleasures; in a word, over a life of secular and finite hopes, in which the true value of the *personal* spirit is sacrificed. Christ is the king of the world to come, of the eternal hopes of the true self-realization, only accomplished by self-restriction in this lower sphere. The future glory cannot be gained save by abandonment of present attractions: even the beauty of the world is a snare, and the dominant idea of morality is asceticism. Enjoyment of the one is incompatible with attainment of the other ('and likewise Lazarus evil things: but now he is comforted, and thou art tormented'). There are then two classes in this Subordinate Dualism: the secularists, who seek impatiently to gratify what they falsely believe to be their true personality, untrusting in a divine purpose in things, extending beyond the visible; and the citizens of the City of Truth, an inheritance won by patient waiting and a resolute sacrifice, not indeed of self, but of the lower instincts, which we must learn to discard, selling all for the one pearl of great price[1]. And these two classes arise by no summary fiat of a divine separation, but by free choice, exercised with full chances in a world of opposites.

PART III.

CITATIONS FROM THE CLEMENTINE HOMILIES.

II. 15. God in His own Nature is one, but His manifestation is twofold, and by means of opposites: Εἷς ὢν αὐτὸς διχῶς καὶ ἐναντίως διεῖλε πάντα τὰ τῶν ἄκρων. The same notion differently expressed, ἀπ' ἀρχῆς αὐτὸς εἷς ὢν καὶ μόνος θεὸς ποιήσας οὐρανὸν καὶ γῆν, ἡμέραν καὶ νύκτα . . . ζωὴν καὶ θάνατον. In the midst of this world of contraries man is placed to exercise free choice on things *already* good and bad (but only

---

[1] MANILIUS IV. 404:—
  Quid caelo dabimus? quantum est, quo veneat omne?
  Impendendus homo est, Deus esse ut possit in ipso.

relatively to him): ᾧ καὶ τὰς τῶν συζυγιῶν ἐνήλλαξεν εἰκόνας. The *present* world is, as it were, the lesser mystery (τὰ μικρά); it is πρόσκαιρος and is full of ἄγνοια; it is θῆλυς and bears children, not for itself but for eternity. The future world is τὰ μείζω, ἀΐδιος, γνῶσις, and ὡς πατὴρ ἀποδεχόμενος its offspring now grown to maturity, from the hands of this age, a mother or a nurse, to whom the early care, but not the complete education, is entrusted. 16. Ἐν ἀρχῇ ὁ Θεὸς εἷς ὤν, ὥσπερ δεξιὰ καὶ ἀριστερά, πρῶτον ἐποίησε τὸν οὐρανὸν εἶτα τὴν γῆν καὶ οὕτως ἐξῆς πάσας τὰς συζυγίας. But in the case of man he *alters* the *order* of this manifestation in pairs. In this way the author marks the difference of man from other creatures (μόνος αὐτεξούσιος) and of the development in History from that of Nature. ἐπὶ μέντοι ἀνθρώπων οὐκέτι οὕτως ἀλλὰ πάσας ἐναλλάττει τὰς συζυγίας. ὡς γὰρ ἀπ' αὐτοῦ τὰ πρῶτα κρείττονα, τὰ δεύτερα ἥττονα (here is a doctrine at the root of all Gnostic Emanationism), ἐπ' ἀνθρώπων τὸ ἐνάντιον εὑρίσκομεν, τὰ πρῶτα χείρονα, τὰ δεύτερα κρείττονα. It is probable that *physical* excellence gives its best first; but the idea of gradual progress seems inseparable from the idea of *moral* perfection. The rejection of evil implies the possibility of yielding to its enticements; and in a measure even this yielding is a necessary moment in an upward course. But it is in vain that we look for steady consistency; 33. *two* new discrepancies arise: ἡ Κακία appears as a personal power, rival of God; and the antecedence of good in physical creation seems abandoned: ἐπεὶ γάρ, ὡς ἔφαμεν, δυϊκῶς καὶ ἐναντίως πάντα ἔχοντα ὁρῶμεν, first Night then Day (but see above), first ignorance then knowledge, first disease then healing,—so πρῶτα τὰ τῆς Πλάνης τῷ βίῳ ἔρχεται, and then Truth, first the diseases by Aaron's rod, then the cure by Moses; (and at this juncture in the struggle of the world), as the pagans are turning from their idols, so ἡ Κακία πάλιν ὡς αὐτὴ βασιλεύουσα anticipates their conversion, and sends forth her guileful favourite, Simon. So III. 59. Προλαβοῦσα ἡ Κακία τῷ τῆς συζυγίας νόμῳ προἀπέστειλε Σίμωνα, to make man believe in many gods, instead of one Creator of the world. So VII. 11 of Simon: αὐτὸς ἐστὶ Μαγός, αὐτὸς διάβολος, αὐτὸς Κακίας ὑπηρέτης. (As to this mysterious prosopopoeia, is it not possible that the writer, struggling with a *moral* conception of sin expressed in language which often reduces it to an original and therefore *physical* distinction, intended by ἡ Κακία, the feminine principle of weakness in created things, aspiring blindly to a fuller participation in its Creator, or, to put it from the Platonic and impersonal point of view, the visible and transient world, striving by ceaseless reproduction of types to appropriate the perfection of the intellectual region—τὰ νοητά? But the theologian must make up his mind whether he will consider this weakness which thwarts, a *defiance* of the Creator's designs, or a *conscious infirmity* which seeks to heal itself. On the answer will depend the entire conception of sin as *physical* or *moral*; and also the notion of God, as interested Creator or impersonal reservoir of goodness. Is Matter to blame for its defects? PLATO inclines to the belief that it is; ARISTOTLE defends it by the new doctrine of the 'yearnings' of inanimate nature (a notion which, though an indefensible personification, lies behind much Pantheistic speculation, notably that of M. VACHEROT). But all this inconsistency merely proves the futility of the Manichean *physical* hypothesis, and its extreme superficiality.)

III. 33. The duplicity of the universe is represented here in a purely *physical* light. God, who creates the world and disposes the elements, makes the pleasure of existence (and perhaps also its duration) to depend upon the law of interaction and alternation. It was perhaps impossible to conceive of the continuance of creation, save under the idea of a perpetual overcoming of an opposite in a new unity: Οὗτος μόνος τὴν μίαν καὶ πρώτην μονοειδῆ οὐσίαν τετραχῶς καὶ ἐναντίως ἔτρεψεν· εἶτα μίξας, κράσεις ἐξ αὐτῶν ἐποίησεν, ἵνα εἰς ἐναντίας φύσεις τετραμμέναι καὶ μεμιγμέναι τοῦ ζῆν ἡδονὴν ἐκ τῆς ἀντισυζυγίας ἐργάσωνται. There is a trace here of a fatal tendency to transform bad and good in man into a mere *physical* distinction of sex in common with earlier speculators; and in this semi-Platonic passage, which recalls both the Symposium and the Timaeus, there is a postulate of Matter coexisting with God which is not explained satisfactorily either here or elsewhere in the *Homilies*.

But from such *metaphysical* or *physical* ideas the writer hastens back to his *personal* relations, the notion of the Two Kingdoms of Darkness and Light, between which man is placed: XV. 7. ὁ τῆς Ἀληθείας παρὼν προφήτης ἐδίδαξεν ἡμᾶς, ὅτι ὁ τῶν ὅλων Δημιουργὸς καὶ Θεός, δυσί τισιν ἀπένειμε βασιλείας δύο, Ἀγαθῷ τε καὶ Πονηρῷ, δοὺς τῷ μὲν Κακῷ τοῦ παρόντος κόσμου μετὰ νόμον τὴν βασιλείαν, ὥστ' ἂν ἔχειν ἐξουσίαν κολάζειν τοὺς ἀδικοῦντας. Τῷ δὲ Ἀγαθῷ τὸν ἐσόμενον ἀίδιον αἰῶνα. In § 6 we have a kind of apologue of these two kingdoms, as of δύο ἐχθρῶν βασιλέων ὄντων καὶ διῃρημένας τὰς χώρας ἐχόντων. Men are defrauders of their true sovereign, so as to live in a foe's land (καθὸ ἐν ἑτέρου εἰσὶ βασιλείᾳ), but God is kind and pardons them. XX. 2. ὁ Θεὸς δύο βασιλείας ὁρίσας καὶ δύο αἰῶνας συνεστήσατο, κρίνας τῷ Πονηρῷ δέδοσθαι τὸν παρόντα κόσμον διὰ τὸ μικρόν τε αὐτὸν εἶναι καὶ παρέρχεσθαι ὄξεως, τῷ δὲ Ἀγαθῷ σώσειν ὑπέσχετο τὸν μέλλοντα αἰῶνα, ἅτε δὴ μέγαν ὄντα καὶ ἀίδιον. Between these man is absolutely free to choose: Τὸν οὖν ἄνθρωπον αὐτεξούσιον ἐποίησεν, ἐπιτηδειότητα ἔχοντα νεύειν πρὸς ἃς βούλεται πράξεις ... ὡς εἶναι τὸν ἄνθρωπον ἐκ φυραμάτων δύο, θηλείας τε καὶ ἄρρενος; and thus, XIX. 23. ὁ κόσμος ὄργανόν ἐστι τεχνικῶς γεγονός, ἵνα τῷ ἐσομένῳ ἄρρενι αἰωνίως ἡ θήλεια τίκτῃ δικαίους αἰωνίους υἱούς. XX. 2. cont.: Διὸ δὴ καὶ δύο ὁδοὶ προετέθησαν, νόμου τε καὶ ἀνομίας· δύο τε βασιλεῖαι ὡρίσθησαν, ἡ μὲν οὐρανῶν λεγομένων, ἡ δὲ τῶν ἐπὶ γῆς νῦν βασιλευόντων. Ἀλλὰ καὶ δύο βασιλεῖς ἐτάχθησαν, ὧν ὁ μὲν τοῦ παρόντος καὶ προσκαίρου κόσμου νόμῳ βασιλεύειν ἐχειροτονήθη ... ὁ δὲ ἕτερος καὶ αὐτὸς βασιλεὺς ὑπάρχων τοῦ ἐσομένου αἰῶνος, στέργει πᾶσαν ἀνθρώπων φύσιν ἐν τοῖς παροῦσι τὴν παρρησίαν ἔχειν οὐ δυνάμενος ἀλλ' ὥς τίς ποτ' ἐστι λανθάνειν πειρώμενος τὰ συμφέροντα συμβουλεύει. (Now it is evident that this writing is an attempt to escape from Gnosticism by the employment of Gnostic resource. With a strong insistence on God as the good Creator of the visible world, a defence indeed of the Creator from the attacks of the prevailing Discontent, the practical ethics amount to a completely Manichean and ascetic repudiation of this life: and, in this passage of Peter's esoteric teaching, this strange Gnostic position is adopted, so strenuously attacked by the orthodox writers, that Christ comes secretly to win men away by stealth from their allegiance. Our legitimate ruler and sovereign is the Devil, or rather this world belongs to him. Does it not appear an infringement of the original partition of Time and Eternity (the temporal and the immortal life), if the Saviour robs the Devil of his subjects before their period of servitude is over?) III. 19. Christ suffered and died here: μέλλοντος αἰῶνος βασιλεὺς εἶναι κατηξιωμένος πρὸς τὸν νῦν ἐμπροθέσμως παρειληφότα νόμῳ τὴν βασιλείαν [τὴν μαχὴν ἐποιεῖτο?]

Each man is free to choose his leader: ἑαυτὸν (XV. 7) ἀπονέμειν ᾧ βούλεται ἢ τῷ παρόντι Κακῷ ἢ τῷ μέλλοντι Ἀγαθῷ. Those who choose the *present* good are richly dowered here (πλουτεῖν τρυφᾶν ἥδεσθαι· τῶν γὰρ ἐσομένων ἀγαθῶν οὐδὲν ἕξουσι). But those who choose the delights of the future kingdom (τὰ τῆς μελλούσης βασιλείας) ... τὰ ἐνταῦθα ὡς ἀλλοτρίου βασιλέως ἴδια ὄντα, αὐτοῖς νομίζεσθαι οὐκ ἔξεστιν, ἢ ὕδατος μόνον καὶ ἄρτου καὶ τούτων μεθ' ἱδρῶτος ποριζομένων πρὸς τὸ ζῆν, καὶ περιβολαίου ἑνός. As in the system of LACTANTIUS, there is no place in the kingdom of God for the wealthy and successful in this life; good fortune here (supposed to be in each case a deliberate choice) disqualifies for eternal bliss: the two spheres are incompatible; and no one can 'make the best of both worlds.'

Daemons have power only over those who yield to their

allurements and eat at their table, VII. 3 : Οὕτω γὰρ ἀπ' ἀρχῆς ὑπὸ τοῦ πάντα κτισάντος Θεοῦ, δυσὶν ἑκάστοτε ἄρχουσι δεξιῷ τε καὶ εὐωνύμῳ ὡρίσθη νόμος μὴ ἔχειν ἑκάτερον αὐτῶν ἐξουσίαν ἐὰν μὴ πρότερόν τινι ὁμοτράπεζος γένηται, ὃν εὖ πυιῆσαι ἢ κακῶσαι βούλεται. And as the fires of Judaic sacrifice are extinguished by the water of Baptism, so the table of Devils (εἰδωλόθυτα) is superseded by the Eucharist. VIII. 21. Christ the king of the future world was exposed to the same temptation, the display of the glories or pleasures, which this life and its prince have to offer : τῷ γὰρ τῆς εὐσεβείας ἡμῶν βασιλεῖ προσῆλθέ ποτε ὁ πρόσκαιρος βασιλεύς, καὶ οὐ βίαν ποιῶν (οὐ γὰρ ἐξῆν) ἀλλὰ προτρέπων καὶ ἀναπείθων (ὅτι τὸ πεισθῆναι ἐπὶ τῇ ἑκάστου κεῖται ἐξουσίᾳ). Christ refuses, knowing this voluntary choice of the temporal means eternal servitude to the Devil. XX. 3. These two beings ever fight together for the possession of Man's allegiance : τῶν δὲ δύο τούτων ὁ ἕτερος τὸν ἕτερον ἐκβιάζεται Θεοῦ κελευσάντος, and each of us has perfect freedom to obey which he prefers. If the Good, he becomes κτῆμα of the future sovereign, whose kingdom is not from hence ; if the Evil, τοῦ παρόντος γίνεται Πονηροῦ ὑπηρέτημα. Notice the *neuters* : it is suggested that the first effort of deliberate will is alone *free;* afterwards we must abide by the consequence ; ' we are not our own.' And remembering the practical problem of that age, the question of the Realm of Freedom, we may see here that κτῆμα implies no real sacrifice of self, but only a voluntary mancipation to a service which is ' perfect freedom,' in which the *personality* is invigorated, not extinguished.

The so-called gifts of Fortune then come from the Devil, who, as in the old German legends, makes a compact with the soul, and barters a fixed period of earthly success for an eternal slavery. But occasionally (and as a result of an inconsistency to which I must again refer) the Devil is represented as punishing his subjects even in this life, ὃς (XX. 3) δι' ἁμαρτίας κρίσει δικαίᾳ τὴν κατ' αὐτοῦ λαβὼν ἐξουσίαν, καὶ πρὸ τοῦ μέλλοντος αἰῶνος θελήσας αὐτῇ χρῆσθαι, ἐν τῷ νῦν βίῳ κολάζων ἥδεται: in which simple sentence lies the whole problem of the alternative, *rebel* or *minister?* and the entire confusion in this writer's mind between indignation at evil and rejoicing in it.

This strife of the two kings, present and to come, constitutes the world-process, or at least the historic development of mankind. Adam is the first manifestation of the good principle. and it is an error to suppose that he fell : III. 22. πλὴν τούτῳ σύζυγος συνεκτίσθη θήλεια φύσις, as inferior to him as μετουσία to οὐσία, as moon to sun, as fire to light. This wife of Adam, who almost approaches the traditional conception of Lilith, is believed to be πρώτη προφῆτις, τοῦ νῦν κόσμου ὡς θήλεια ὁμοίου ἄρχουσα. II. 16. From Adam there arose, first ἄδικος Καΐν, second δίκαιος Ἀβέλ, according to the law of Emanation (ὁ λόγος, or ὁ κανὼν τῆς συζυγίας, or (III. 23) κατὰ τὸν τῆς προόδου λόγον, and ἐν τῇ τῶν συζυγιῶν προελεύσει). Symbolical of this great secret, now at last revealed, is the emission of the birds from Noah's ark. II. 16. cont.: πνευμάτων εἰκόνες δύο ἀπεστάλησαν ἀκαθάρτου λέγω καὶ καθαροῦ, first the black raven, then the white dove. We have the pairs: Ishmael, Isaac ; Esau, Jacob ; Aaron (τῇ τάξει πρῶτος ... ὁ ἀρχιερεύς· εἶτα ὁ νομοθέτης), Moses. The last pair that preceded Simon Magus and Peter were Jesus and John the Baptist (II. 17, III. 22), last representative of the female principle: ὁ ἐν γεννητοῖς γυναικῶν πρῶτος ἦλθεν, εἶτα ὁ ἐν υἱοῖς ἀνθρώπων. So II. 23, of John: ὃς καὶ τοῦ κυρίου ... κατὰ τὸν τῆς συζυγίας λόγον ἐγένετο πρόοδος. In like manner the Magus precedes Peter: II. 17. ὁ πρὸ ἐμοῦ εἰς τὰ ἔθνη πρῶτος ἐλθών (repeated III. 59). 'It is easy to detect whose he is, and whose am I,' ὁ μετ' ἐκεῖνον ἐληλυθὼς ... ὡς σκότῳ φῶς, ὡς ἀγνοίᾳ γνῶσις, ὡς νόσῳ ἴασις. So, as Christ said, first must come the false gospel ὑπὸ πλάνου τινός, then, to cleanse the holy place, must the true gospel be secretly dispensed (κρυφὰ διαπεμφθῆναι εἰς ἐπανόρθωσιν τῶν ἐσομένων αἱρέσεων). At the end of the world comes Antichrist and Christ, at whose advent all the works

Subordinate Dualism. 165

of darkness shall become invisible (ἀφανῆ). The source of error in man is ignorance of this Canon of Dualism. II. 18. ἐπεὶ οὖν, ὡς ἔφην, τὸν Κανόνα τῆς Συζυγίας ἀγνοοῦσί τινες, so the character and origin of Simon Magus is not rightly known. Νῦν δὲ ἀγνοούμενος, οὐκ ὀρθῶς πιστεύεται.

In such a system, then, everything is adapted and arranged for the trial and probation of man the individual. Punishment is corrective and admonitory, and aims at the restoration of the sinner (XII. 32): it is not GOD's will that he should be unhappy, but the inevitable result of his own free choice. GOD forces none to obey and love him. All trials and diseases in life have this single object, the testing of the Saints, who give up, with prudent foresight and sincere faith in GOD's promises, the pleasures of the present world. In opposition to the enemies of Providence (that much impugned doctrine in this period; compare LACTANTIUS), it is maintained that not the smallest thing happens without GOD; and thus it must be confessed that the writer has caught hold of the main teaching of Christianity from its human side; the extension of the idea of Πρόνοια from *national* or *cosmic* to *individual* life. Much the same principle underlies this sentence (XII. 32): Δίκαιος δέ ἐστιν ἐκεῖνος ὁ τοῦ εὐλόγου ἕνεκα τῇ φύσει μαχόμενος, for merit resides not in letter of scripture or in verbal obedience, but in the innate sense of right and wrong, and the cultivation of moral spontaneity.

PART IV.

More particular account of the origin of Evil in the CLEMENTINE HOMILIES.

§ 1. From the standpoint of human nature, based on the value of the *personal* will and free choice, the evil in the world is capable of explanation. The *Moral* difficulties vanish, to a great extent, if we may assume a rival principle to the will of GOD, who seeks to divert us from thoughts on our true home, Eternity, and who already anticipates our appearance in the world by his opposition to GOD (merely transient and fictitious though it may perhaps be). Our *moral* nature implies choice; but choice implies opposites and contraries; thus nothing, not our pain, or success, or disease or health, or poverty or riches, falls outside the counsels of GOD, who tries, by means of His two servants, of what temper we are. Thus, from an *ethical* point of view, we may silence our doubts; for it would be difficult to imagine a *moral* world except in this way; but the *speculative* problems as to the origin and nature of the Evil One remain unsolved. In the Homilies Books XIX and XX are given up to this discussion, which is significantly omitted in the *later* Recognitions.

There are two arguments, one with Simon in XIX, the other with the believing disciples in XX. Simon is an adversary whose main object is to perplex, and it is difficult to form an accurate idea of his doctrine. At first he wishes to shift the responsibility of evil from the Devil to his Creator. 'Who is the Evil One?' I do not know, but believe that he exists, as Christ told us: διὸ κἀγὼ σύμφημι αὐτὸν ὑπάρχειν. 'Is he create or uncreate? (γενητός, ἀγένητος), for if we discover his author, we shall transfer the blame.' Not so, for perhaps GOD cannot prevent it, εἰ δὲ οὐδ' αὐτὸς δυνατός, κρείττων ὁ πρὸς τῷ ἀδυνατεῖν κατὰ τὸ δυνατὸν εὐεργετεῖν ἡμᾶς οὐκ ὀκνῶν. [Here Peter approaches the position of J. S. MILL.] Even if created by GOD, GOD is not blameworthy, for good men have bad sons. He is created, but does not receive his evil from GOD; and yet we must allow that nothing happens contrary to GOD's will, Who (§ 12) can be προβολεὺς ... τῶν τεσσάρων οὐσιῶν, θερμοῦ λέγω καὶ ψυχροῦ, ὑγροῦ τε καὶ ξηροῦ. At first they were simple: ὡς πρῶτα ἁπλῆ καὶ ἀμιγῆ ὄντα πρὸς οὐδέτερον ἔχειν τὴν ὄρεξιν, προβληθέντα δὲ ὑπὸ τοῦ Θεοῦ καὶ ἔξω κραθέντα γένεσθαι ζῷον, προαίρεσιν ἔχον ὀλοθρεῦσαι κακούς (a). Inasmuch as all these are born from GOD, ὁ Πονηρὸς οὔτ' ἀλλοθέν ἐστιν, οὔτ' ἀπ' αὐτοῦ ... Θεοῦ τὴν κακίαν εἴληφε, because these οὐσίαι

Subordinate Dualism.

in themselves at first neither bad nor good, οὐθέτεραι οὖσαι πεφυλοκρινημέναι ἐξ αὐτοῦ προβέβληνται, καὶ ἔξω αὐταῖς κραθείσαις ὑπὸ τῆς αὐτοῦ τέχνης, βουλήσει (= *voluntario motu*?) συμβέβηκεν ἡ πρὸς τὸν τῶν κακῶν ὄλεθρον ἐπιθυμία (b). Here appears the inconsistency of a proposed explanation, half *physical*, half *moral*; and again, this conception of the Devil as the willing minister of GOD's righteous judgements, is quite incomplete, and takes no notice of the element of *moral* perversion, being little more than PHILO's notion of the βασιλικὴ δύναμις. This view is rejected by Simon: Δυνατὸς οὖν ὑπάρχων ὁ Θεὸς κιρνᾶν τὰ στοιχεῖα, καὶ ποιεῖν κράσεις, πρὸς ἃς βούλεται γένεσθαι προαιρέσεις, διὰ τί μὴ ἐποίει ἀγαθῶν προαιρετικὴν τὴν ἑκάστου κρᾶσιν; (a question which is always being asked in some form). Peter at last grants that this peculiar temper of the Devil arose in accordance with GOD's will: οὕτως βουλῇ τοῦ συγκιρνάντος συμβέβηκεν ὡς ἠθέλησεν ἡ τῶν Κακῶν προαίρεσις (c). Here is clearly an inconsistency: the Devil passes from antagonism to GOD into the position of an agent.

In § 14 Simon suggests an honest Dualism of GOD and Matter: τί δὲ εἰ ἡ Ὕλη αὐτῷ σύγχρονος οὖσα καὶ ἰσοδύναμος ὡς ἐχθρὰ προβάλλει αὐτῷ ἡγεμόνας ἐμποδίζοντας αὐτοῦ τοῖς βουλήμασι; so again, § 17: Μήτι ἀεὶ ὢν καὶ οὕτως ἀναιρεῖται τὰ τῆς Μοναρχίας, συναρχούσης καὶ ἑτέρας τῆς κατὰ τὴν Ὕλην δυνάμεως[1]; There are two ways of regarding the material substrate, as *limiting* or *aspiring after* the good, or the intellectual world. PLUTARCH, in his 'Isis and Osiris,' adopts the former view (both are possible in Platonic thought), and is almost tempted to personify the *weakness* of the receptive element into obstinate rebellion.

This Peter denies; Matter recognizes and obeys GOD, and Jesus in the miracles shows His power over it. Simon wishes to press Peter to one of two conclusions; either we start from

---

[1] Dressel's translation here quite misses the point, and is ungrammatical. For use of μήτί γε = nonne (hypothetical and suggestive), see XX. 9 (ad fin.).

GOD's omnipotence, and believe him to be the Author of Evil; or preferring to connect the Divine Nature rather with *goodness* than *power*, we suppose Matter to be almost independent of this authority. 'If GOD ensouled Matter, ἐνεψύχωσεν αὐτὴν οὐκ αὐτὸς αἴτιός ἐστιν ὧν αὐτὴ τίκτει κακῶν;' Peter replies with a compendium of orthodox doctrine: 'all earthly evils arise because of man's fall' (ἕρπετα ἰόβολα, βοταναὶ θανάσιμοι, and Daemons); 'and if you ask why man was thus made capable of death, I respond because he is free (αὐτεξούσιος).'

§ 16. Nor is GOD unjust, if he makes use of the Devil's malice for his own righteous ends: εἰ ἀποστάντα αὐτὸν ὁ Θεὸς ἄρχειν τῶν ὁμοίων κατέστησε νόμῳ, τὴν τιμωρίαν ἐπάγειν τοῖς ἁμαρτάνουσι κελεύσας αὐτῷ, οὐκ ἄδικός ἐστιν. § 17. Simon, thinking more of his *opposition* to GOD than his *ministry*, asks: why εἰδὼς αὐτὸν ἐπὶ κακῷ ἐσόμενον, γινόμενον αὐτὸν οὐκ ἀνεῖλε; § 18. Simon starts a third possible theory, taking its origin from pantheism: Evil only relative: Μήτι οὖν τῶν πρός τί ἐστιν; depends on its *object* for its qualification: in this way all distinctions vanish; evil is not evil, nor is good, good; all is in Heraclitean flux: ἑκάτερον γὰρ θάτερον ἐργάζεται. So, § 19: Μήτι οὖν οὐκ ἔστι τῇ φύσει πονηρὸν ἢ ἀγαθόν, ἀλλὰ νόμῳ διαφέρει καὶ ἔθει; that is, the Source of Life, physical or mental, is indifferent; and all morality grows up by convention, and depends on institutions which are only locally valid.

In § 20 Peter introduces a new idea—Sin neither truly existent nor eternal: οὐκ ἄρα ὑπάρχει τὸ Πονηρὸν ἀεί, ἀλλ' οὐδὲ μὴν ὑπάρξαι δύναται.

The rest of this book XIX is occupied with Simon's gnostic attacks on the evils, cruelty, inequality of this world; and shows clearly how entirely the early heresies depended upon this widespread Discontent, whether it were *practical* or *speculative* Peter replies: 'Much physical evil in the world arises from our carelessness, from neglect of the rules of health or the fitting periods of generation. And besides, pains here are to correct sin, and to lead away from ignorance: if you are good, you will not suffer: δὸς τὸν μὴ ἁμαρτάνοντα καὶ λαβὲ τὸν μὴ πάσχοντα. This is very inconsistent; here pain, instead of being a *probation*, is a *retribution*. But the position of the former books is that pain in this life is the inseparable lot of those who choose eternal happiness. 'As to the terrible injustice and inequality of life, it is necessary for the perfection of saints; some by suffering, others by seizing an occasion of charity, are made pious (εὐσεβεῖς ἀποτελεσθῆναι).' Simon departs, after an angry reply and an indignant and somewhat modern protest, that in this theory the poor are a mere instrument for the perfection of the wealthy.

In the next book Peter undertakes privately to explain the truth τῆς περὶ τοῦ Πονηροῦ ἁρμονίας. The Devil is the duly appointed king of the present world, ὃς καὶ ἐπ' ὀλέθρῳ πονηρῶν χαίρειν ἐκράθη (d). Now this feeling, though in itself not commendable, is used by GOD, who cannot punish sinners directly: καὶ ὡς ἰδίᾳ χαριζόμενος ἐπιθυμίᾳ τὴν τοῦ Θεοῦ βούλησιν ἐκτελεῖ. Christ on the other hand is *created* (δημιουργηθείς) to rejoice in authority over the good, and saves them to eternal life, ἑαυτῷ χαριζόμενος τὴν ὑπὲρ τούτων εἰς Θεὸν ἀναφέρει χάριν. Both please themselves, but in doing so serve GOD; and both are ministers and agents of GOD's good pleasure: οἱ δύο ἡγεμόνες οὗτοι ταχεῖαι χεῖρες εἰσὶ Θεοῦ προλαμβάνειν ἐπιθυμοῦσαι καὶ τὸ αὐτοῦ θέλημα ἐπιτελεῖν· even now desirous of anticipating the *pains* of the wicked, the *delights* of the just. It is GOD who really acts throughout; He kills and makes alive: ἀποκτείνει μὲν διὰ τῆς ἀριστερᾶς ... διὰ τοῦ ἐπὶ κακώσει τῶν ἀσεβῶν χαίρειν κραθέντος Πονηροῦ. σώζει δὲ καὶ εὐεργετεῖ διὰ τῆς δεξιᾶς ... διὰ τοῦ ἐπ' εὐεργεσίᾳ καὶ σωτηρίᾳ δικαίων χαίρειν δημιουργηθέντος Ἀγαθοῦ.

XX. 3. Εἰσὶ δὲ οὗτοι τὰς οὐσίας ἔχοντες οὐκ ἔξωθεν τοῦ Θεοῦ, οὐδὲ γάρ ἐστιν ἑτέρα τις ἀρχή ... οὐ μὴν ἀπὸ τοῦ Θεοῦ ὡς ζῷα προεβλήθησαν· ὁμόδοξοι γὰρ αὐτῷ ἦσαν ... οὔτε συμβεβήκασιν αὐτομάτως, παρὰ τὴν αὐτοῦ βουλὴν γεγονότες, ἐπεὶ τὸ τῆς δυνάμεως

Subordinate Dualism.

αὐτοῦ μέγιστον ἀνῄρητο ἄν, ... ἀλλ' ἀπὸ τοῦ Θεοῦ μὲν προβέ-βληται τὰ πρώτιστα στοιχεῖα τέσσαρα (warm, cold, wet, dry, or fire, air, water, earth). Whence GOD is the Father of all existence (ὅθεν δὴ καὶ Πατὴρ τυγχάνει πάσης οὐσίας,—οὔσης γνώμης τῆς κατὰ τὴν κρᾶσιν (His plan as to the mixture of elements taking effect?) The materials or elements of creation then come from GOD himself by *projection*: His design as to their commingling and permeation then takes effect. Yet out of this purely *physical* conception arises, by a sudden turn, the idea of *moral* difference: ἔξω γὰρ κραθεῖσιν αὐτοῖς ὡς τέκνον ἡ Προαίρεσις ἐγεννήθη. And so the Devil is really only a *minister* of GOD, and is blameless: ὁ οὖν Πονηρὸς πρὸς τῷ τοῦ ἐνεστῶτος κόσμου τέλει ὑπουργήσας ἀμέμπτως τῷ Θεῷ (ἅτε δὴ οὐ μιᾶς οὐσίας ὢν τῆς πρὸς κακίαν μόνης), μετασυγ-κριθεὶς ἀγαθὸς γένεσθαι δύναται. οὐδὲ γὰρ νῦν κακόν τι ποιεῖ, καίτοι Κακὸς ὤν, νομίμως κακουχεῖν εἰληφὼς τὴν ἐξουσίαν. This universalist and Origenian doctrine on the return of Satan to his allegiance, seems to depend upon a dim adumbration of modern science: thought is molecular displacement, and character depends upon a particular arrangement of atoms. And it is quite obvious that this writer who insists most strongly on *human* freedom and responsibility, shrinks from attributing the same liberty to the Evil angels, i.e. is reduced to a *physical* instead of an *ethical* explanation.)

XX. 5. Sophonias states an article of his belief which strikes at the entire Gnostic doctrine of Emanation and successive Deterioration: τὸ μὲν γεννῆσαι (Θεὸν) δίδωμι, τὸ δὲ ἀνόμοιον αὐτῷ γεννῆσαι οὐκ ἀποδίδωμι. Peter becomes pensive at this (ἐπὶ συννοίας γενόμενος), and repents of having begun this inextricable discussion, and sets forth a vague theory of GOD's power to 'change' things, even Himself.

Ὁ μὲν προβάλλων καὶ εἰς ἑτέραν οὐσίαν τραπέντα πάλιν ἐφ' ἑαυτὸν τρέπειν δύναται, ὁ δὲ προβληθεὶς τῆς ἐξ ἐκείνου τροπῆς ... τέκνον ὑπάρχων, ἄνευ τοῦ προβάλλοντος βουλῆς ἄλλο τι γενέσθαι οὐ δύναται, εἰ μὴ ἐκεῖνος θέλει. Thus the Devil *is exactly what*

Subordinate Dualism.

GOD *wishes him to be*, and cannot overpower the law of his own nature and conformation. XX. 8. Michaiah asks if the Good spirit γεγένηται like the Evil? If so, they seem to be brothers. Peter replies: οὐχ ὁμοίως γεγόνασιν... τοῦ Πονηροῦ ἡ τετραγένης τοῦ σώματος οὐσία πεφυλοκρινημένη ὑπὸ τοῦ Θεοῦ προεβλήθη, ἔξω δὲ αὐτῆς κατὰ τὴν τοῦ προβάλοντος βουλὴν ἐκράθη πρὸς τὴν κρᾶσιν ἡ κακοῖς χαίρουσα προαίρεσις (e). (It appears then that GOD is the author of so-called Evil, by deliberate creation or projection of elements so mingled, that a certain ἕξις necessarily came upon them, and will continue until the component parts are redistributed.) But this hypothesis is not readily accepted: διὰ τί δὲ ἔξω ὑπ' αὐτοῦ κραθείσης οὐσίας ἡ συμβεβηκυῖα κακοῖς χαίρουσα προαίρεσις ἐπεγίνετο (f); For as to the 'Evil' Will (whatever the exact sense of 'Evil'):

> οὔτε ὑπὸ τοῦ Θεοῦ γεγέννηται,
> οὔτε ὑφ' ἑτέρου τινος,
> οὔτε ὑφ' αὐτοῦ προβέβληται,
> οὔτε αὐτομάτως προελήλυθεν,
> οὔτε ἀεὶ ἦν (ὡς ἡ πρὸ τῆς συγκράσεως οὐσία),

ἀλλὰ κατὰ τὴν τοῦ Θεοῦ βούλησιν ἔξω τῇ κράσει συμβέβηκεν. Ὁ δὲ Ἀγαθὸς ἐκ τῆς τοῦ Θεοῦ καλλίστης τροπῆς γεννηθεὶς καὶ οὐκ ἔξω κράσει συμβεβηκὼς τῷ ὄντι Ὑιός ἐστιν. It cannot be denied that we have here the worst features of the Necessitarian and Impersonal view of GOD, which lies at the root of Gnosticisms. In this difficulty the writer flies to a refuge which he had once abandoned with contempt—the letter of Scripture: ἐπεὶ ταῦτα ἄγραφα τυγχάνει καὶ στοχασμοῖς πεπιστωμένα, μὴ πάντως ἡμῖν οὕτως ἔχειν βεβαιούσθω (compare ORIGEN, who imposes a similar condition on his speculation in his 'Principia'; and it may here be remarked that the Doctrine of Reserve, so generally supposed to be the edifice of aristocratic pride and intellectualism, may with equal likelihood be founded on humility: the ἀπορρήτων εὕρεσις is not *certain* and therefore cannot be communicated to all men as authoritative Dogma).

But a still more complete exculpation of the Devil awaits us; in XX. 9, Lazarus now boldly puts a question, which has been on our tongues for some time past: Πῶς δυνατὸν εὔλογον εἶναι τὸν ὑπὸ Θεοῦ δικαίου καταστάντα Πονηρὸν ὥστε ἀσεβησάντων εἶναι τιμωρόν, τοῦτον αὐτὸν ὕστερον μετὰ τῶν αὐτοῦ ἀγγέλων σὺν τοῖς ἁμαρτωλοῖς εἰς τὸ σκότος τὸ κατώτερον πέμπεσθαι; there remains, then, to sever the notion of pain from the Devil's sojourn in Hell; for the Devil is an Angel who *fears* GOD, *performs* His will, and *punishes* His traitors. Peter: Κἀγὼ ὁμολογῶ ὅτι ὁ Πονηρὸς πονηρὸν οὐδὲν ποιεῖ, καθὸ τὸν δοθέντα αὐτῷ νόμον ἐκτελεῖ. Καίτοι προαίρεσιν ἔχων κακὴν ὅμως φόβῳ τῷ πρὸς τὸν Θεὸν οὐδὲν ἀδίκως πράσσει (notice that προαίρεσις has now lost its true *personal* and *ethical* significance, and is confused with the necessary result of a certain mixture of elements). Διαβάλλων δὲ διδασκάλους ἀληθείας εἰς ἐνέδραν τῶν ἀκριτῶν καὶ διάβολος ὁ αὐτὸς ὀνομάζεται.—To this conclusion there is but one corollary, a modified belief in 'happiness in Hell.' Ὁ Πονηρὸς σκότῳ χαίρειν κατὰ τὴν κρᾶσιν γεγονώς, μετὰ τῶν ὁμοδούλων ἀγγέλων εἰς τὸ τοῦ Ταρτάρου σκότος κατελθὼν ἥδεται· φίλον γὰρ πυρὶ τὸ σκότος. Whereas men's souls, φωτὸς καθαροῦ σταγόνες οὖσαι, are punished in such environment. Thus it is clear that man's spiritual nature differs from the devil's, and in reality only the former is free, the latter being *physically* so compounded that his character is foredetermined and is not the result of free-will. If he were not thus sent into darkness, τότε οὐ δύναται ἡ κακοῖς αὐτοῦ χαίρουσα κρᾶσις μετασυγκριθῆναι εἰς ἀγαθοῦ προαίρεσιν (?) (f). (This sentence is very ambiguous, but seems to imply a future change in his temper when his work of *thwarting, chastising, deceiving*, in accordance with GOD's will shall be over.) Καὶ οὕτως ἀγαθὸς (? ἀγαθοῖς) συνεῖναι κριθήσεται ταύτῃ μᾶλλον, ὅτι κακοῖς χαίρουσαν λελογχὼς κρᾶσιν (g), αἰτίᾳ τοῦ πρὸς τὸν Θεὸν φόβου οὐδὲν παρὰ τὸ δοκοῦν τῷ τοῦ Θεοῦ νόμῳ διεπράξατο. May not, he asks, the story of the change of Aaron's rod into a snake and back again into a rod be a foreshadowing in mystic language of the Devil's altered character? (τὴν τοῦ Πονηροῦ ὕστερον γενησομένην τῆς τροπῆς μετασύγκρασιν.)

PART V.

THE RECOGNITIONS.

IN this somewhat more orthodox recension, we have the same doctrine of the two kingdoms, to be chosen by the free-will of each.

Duo regna constituit Deus et principes emisit: unum saeculare et praesenti voluptatis praemio coronatum; alterum, fide prehensum sed aeternam mercedem pollicens. Hic boni male habentur; et pessimus quisque insultat melioribus:—ita dubitari non potest, reservari utrumque in meritorum suorum compensationem. This is the *moral* distinction of the two realms of time and eternity; (so I. 24 *Duo regna posuit praesentis dico temporis et futuri*): but we have besides the *physical* distinction: I. 27 *Ita totius Mundi machinam, cum una domus esset, in duas dividit regiones. Divisionis autem haec fuit causa, ut superna regio angelis habitaculum, inferior vero praeberet hominibus:—et sic cuncta praeparata sunt ut hominibus qui habitarent in ea, essent facultas his omnibus pro arbitrio uti, ... sive ad bona velint, sive ad mala.*—III. 52 *Potestatem dedit unicuique arbitrii sui, ut hoc esse possit quod vult, et rursum* praevidens *quia ista potestas arbitrii alios quidem faceret eligere bona, alios vero mala, et per hoc in duos ordines necessario propagandum esset hominum genus,—unicuique ordini concessit et locum et regem, quem vellet eligere; bonus enim rex bonis gaudet, et malignus malis.*—IV. 19 *Est ergo in potestate uniuscuiusque (quia liberi arbitrii factus est homo), utrum nobis* (Apostles) *velit audire ad vitam, an daemonibus ad interitum.*—IV. 25. GOD foresees perversion of His good gift, and arranges accordingly; but this foresight in no way interferes with free choice:—*Praevidit diversos ordines atque officia differentia, ut esset diversitas in ordinibus et officiis, secundum proprios animorum motus, ex arbitrii libertate proferendos.* He thus foresees sin, but does not force thereto: and He prepares a system of corrective punishment for our good:— *Oportuit ergo esse et poenarum ministros, quos tamen arbitrii libertas in hunc ordinem traheret*: besides *debuerunt habere quos vincerent hi qui agones susceperant caelestium praemiorum.*

V. 9 *Qui permanet in malo et servus est Mali, non potest effici portio Boni; quia ab initio, ut ante diximus, duo regna statuit Deus, et potestatem dedit unicuique hominum, ut illius regni fiat portio, cui se ad obedientiam ipse subiecerit.* GOD has clearly defined this: *non posse unum hominem utriusque regni esse servum.*

VIII. 52. How justly GOD succours the corrupt state of the world! *ut quoniam bonis Dei mala (quae ex peccato originem sumpserant) sociata sunt, duabus his partibus duos principes poneret, et ei qui bonis gaudet bonorum ordinem . . . . statuit, ei vero qui malis gaudet, ea quae contra ordinem et inutiliter geruntur (ex quibus sine dubio etiam Providentiae fides in dubium veniat); et habita est per hoc a iusto Deo iusta divisio.*—II. 18. The origin and wiles of the Devil (about which subject the Recognitions observe a certain reticence) are made to depend on Man's need of probation:—*ut ergo infideles a fidelibus, pii discernantur ab impiis, permissum est Maligno uti his artibus, quibus singulorum erga verum parentem probentur affectus.* So § 17 *Studet Inimicus . . . . inimicos eos efficere conditori suo.* III. 55 *Propter hos ergo qui salutis suae neglectu placent Malo, et eos qui studio utilitatis suae placere cupiunt Bono,—paria quaedam ad temptationem praesenti huic saeculo statuta sunt.* § 59 *Paria quaedam huic mundo destinasse Deum; ille qui primus ex paribus venit, a Malo est, qui secundus a Bono*; and every one has a chance of making up his mind (*occasio iudicii*), whether he is foolish

Subordinate Dualism.

and believes the first who comes, or whether, being wise, he is able to discern the Spirits.—§ 61 *Paria . . . . huic mundo destinata sunt ab initio saeculi* :—

Cain.	Abel.
The Giants.	Noah.
Pharaoh.	Abraham.
The Philistines.	Isaac.
Esau.	Jacob.
The Magicians.	Moses.
The Tempter.	The Son of Man.
Simon Magus.	Peter.
(All nations.)	Verbi Seminator (?).
Anti-Christ.	Christ.

There is no intelligible account given of the Fall of Man ; *mundani spiritus* are casually mentioned. I. 42. Daemons clearly exercise a kind of divine commission to try nations and individuals. IV. 33. We overcome them not by our own strength ; *sed propter Dei, qui eos subiecit, potestatem.* —VIII. 50 *(Deus) magis indulsit per singulas gentes angelos quosdam agere principatum, qui malis gaudent.*—We cannot throw the responsibility of our faults on the Devils: II. 18 *Quomodo ergo dicemus Malignum esse causam peccati nostri, quum hoc permissu Dei fiat, ut per ipsum probentur?* and IX. 16, Clement's father sums up the 'sermon' of his son rightly: *cum eo quod inest libertas arbitrii, est extrinsecus et aliqua Causa mali, ex qua per diversas concupiscentias incitantur quidem homines, non tamen coguntur ad peccatum.*

We may ask then, what is Sin? VIII. 51 *Ex arbitrii libertate unusquisque hominum, dum incredulus est de futuris* (that is, about the righteous personality and Providence of GOD, about the purposeful origin and final justice of the world), *per malos actus incurrit in mala* ; and into a superficial, suspicious, and short-sighted philosophy of present enjoyment.—Belief in the Christian message, i.e. in future

judgement and eternal life, cannot come by intellectual process: it is rather an irresistible corollary (compare FICHTE's *Vocation of Man*, Book III). V. 35 *Non aliter scire poteritis* (the truth of our preaching), *nisi ut obedientes his quae mandantur ipso rerum exitu et beatitudinis certissimo fine doceamini*[1].
—The Christian is therefore contrasted with the children of this world: VI. 13 *Debemus praecellere eos, qui praesens tantum saeculum nôrunt*: V. 5 *Pergentibus ad civitatem salutis*. What is meritorious is a belief that the Creator will at last restore the balance of justice: VII. 33 *immortalis et beata vita credentibus danda promittitur*: VIII. 48 *Divina Providentia iudicium erga omnes statuit, quia praesens saeculum non erat tale, in quo unusquisque possit pro meritis dispensari*.

The first impulse of the individual (CLEMENT's ἡ πρώτη νεῦσις πρὸς σωτηρίαν) is curiously defined: III. 53 *Malus . . . . apud Deum qui requirere non vult quod sibi expedit* (probably ὅστις οὐ βούλεται ζητῆσαι τὸ ἑαυτῷ συμφέρον). So VIII. 59 *qui desiderium gerunt cognoscendi quod sibi expedit*. The writer here insists on the primary motive of self-interest; and this is true in a great majority of cases, if we consult history and experience. 'What shall we do to be saved?' It rises from a sense of personal unease and alienation, not, in the first instance, from a vague altruistic sentiment. The soul is for the time alone with GOD, and forgets all else in this solitude. The first gaze of the awakening spirit, now fully self-conscious, is turned within, not without. 'Is thy heart right with My heart?' is the question GOD puts to it. It inquires of itself: 'Do I realize my own dignity and worth in the eyes of GOD?' GOD distinguishes those who seek their own good and their own hurt: *Deus quod utile est* (III. 53) *occultavit hominibus* (i.e. the possession of the kingdom of heaven, or immortal life, which is the only good).

The bad, then, are the lazy; *qui neglexissent quod sibi utile et salutare esset inquirere, tamquam seipsos odio habentes*.

---

[1] Compare also RECOGN. II. 22: III 37. 41, 59.

Those who recognize what is best for them extinguish the flames of the old carnal birth at the font, the second birth by water: IX. 7 *Prima enim nostra nativitas, per* ignem *concupiscentiae descendit, et ideo dispensatione divina, secunda haec per* aquam *introducitur, quae restinguat* ignis *naturam* . . . . (the soul must so live) *ut nullas omnino Mundi huius voluptates requirat, sed sit tamquam peregrinus et advena, atque alterius civitatis civis.*

Nothing can be clearer than this speculative doctrine of man's origin, duty, and destiny. The problem of the author of evil recedes into the background. The 'malign one' and his angels are indeed mentioned as they might be in orthodox Christian writings, but we miss the detailed *metaphysical* inquiry, degenerating into a mere *physical* hypothesis, which occupies the later books of the Homilies. The centre of the system in the 'Recognitions' is the free-will of man the individual, and his instinct of self-preservation, which, by means of corrective discipline (IV. 11, 23) and the probation of daemonic wiles, is educated and developed into a sincere desire for immortal life, an ascetic repudiation of all fictitious worldly delights in this, a determination to regard suffering as chastisement coming from a Father's hand, and a firm trust in GOD's justice and mercy (which does not wait for proof) that all present wrongs will be righted at the Judgement Day.

PART VI.

THE WRITINGS OF FIRMIANUS LACTANTIUS.

THIS last of the Latin writers of the Ante-Nicene Church recalls the author of the *Clementines* in two points; the formal doctrine of the origin and use of evil, and the presence of interpolations which it is difficult to separate from the text. His conception of the world-process may be gathered from the following axioms, which resume the leading features of his doctrine:—

(*a*) He writes to effect a new alliance between *Religio* and *Sapientia*, so long divorced; the one superstitious, the other merely negative and destructive.

(*b*) He is intensely indignant against the Epicureans especially, who deny design; with these pretended philosophers the Christian has nothing in common. All others agree in believing that conscious reason rules the world with deliberate design.

(*c*) There is for the believer a moral and personal Creator; and the purpose of GOD in building the world for us was to put before rational beings the high prize of immortality, to be won at the price of hard toil and frequent probation.

(*d*) To this end He establishes us with free-will in a world of contraries; in the centre between bad and good, higher and lower; creating (?) a leader of the right and a leader of the left, like a constitutional monarch who establishes the useful interaction of rival parties. This GOD does with full fore-knowledge of the corruption and degradation of men.

(*e*) Both come from Him, Who is Almighty, yet chooses to create something that seemingly thwarts His designs. Evil He does not create, so much as '*set before*' man's eyes (*proposuit*). Evil does not then become ethical (that is, really evil) until man chooses; and this word (*proposuit*) reminds one of the continual reference to man's probation: evil in its nature is probably only in *relation* to us. All things are in pairs; a Pythagorean συστοιχία; right and left; heaven and earth; light and darkness; soul and body; and this latter is *bad* in its nature and a hindrance to our better aspirations. Apart from Evil, Good is absolutely inconceivable.

(*f*) The Final Good is clearly Immortal Life, and virtue (conceived of as an objective law) is only the means appointed by GOD whereby we attain to it. Virtue is pure impassibility, the absolute surrender and refusal of all the tempting allurements of this life; success and happiness here is entirely incompatible with future bliss.

This *arcanum* or *sacramentum mundi* is clearly and concisely stated in Epit. 69 *Factus a Deo Mundus, ut homines nascerentur; nascuntur autem homines, ut Deum patrem agnoscant (in quo est Sapientia); agnoscunt ut colant (in quo est Iustitia); colunt ut mercedem Immortalitatis accipiant; accipiunt Immortalitatem ut in aeternum Deo serviant.* Everything is thus referred to the *moral* conception of man, and his perfecting through trial for a future inheritance.

Present interest will centre round (*d*) and (*e*), and the Lactantian idea of duality in this world, which forms the centre of his system (Opif. 10: The nose GOD made *ipsa duplicitate pulcerrimum. Ex quo intelligimus, quantum dualis numerus una et simplici compage solidatus ad veram valeat perfectionem*) . . . . To him *physical* motion and *moral* free-will were alike impossible, unless there existed two extremes, opposite yet in a sense united, each entailing the other, between which a path might be traversed in either direction. And so there is absolute need of antithesis: III. 29 *Ex quo fit, ut virtus nulla sit, nisi adversarius sit.* V. 7 *Virtutem aut cerni non posse, nisi habeat vitia contraria; aut non esse perfectam, nisi exerceatur adversis. Hanc enim Deus bonorum et malorum voluit esse distantiam, ut qualitatem boni ex malo sciamus, &c. . . . . nec alterius ratio intelligi sublato altero potest. Deus ergo non exclusit malum, ut ratio virtutis constare posset.* VI. 22 *At enim saepe dictum est, virtutem nullam futuram fuisse, nisi haberet quae opprimeret.* VII. 4 *Ipsa ratio ac necessitas exigebat et bona homini proponi, et mala; bona quibus utatur, mala quae vitet et caveat.* II. 8 (the interpolator, a somewhat bolder exponent of this theory of Subordinate Dualism): 'Bonum et malum fecit, ut posset esse Virtus, quae nisi malis agitetur, aut vim suam perdet, aut omnino non erit.' (Contrast alone brings our value of goodness and health.) Ita bonum sine malo in hac vita esse non potest. Utrumque, licet contrarium sit, tamen ita cohaeret, ut alterum si tollas, utrumque sustuleris; nam neque bonum comprehendi et percipi potest sine declinatione et fuga mali, nec malum caveri ac vinci sine auxilio comprehensi ac percepti mali. Necesse igitur fuerat, et malum fieri, ut bonum fieret.' VII. 5 (the same later hand), some one asks, 'Cur non bonum tantum fecit, ut nemo peccaret, nemo faceret malum? Nulla .... virtus esse poterat, nisi diversa fecisset, nec omnino apparere vis boni potest, nisi ex mali comparatione.' Evil is nothing but 'boni interpretatio' .... he who instituted the circus-games 'amator unius coloris fuit, sed alterum ei et quasi aemulum posuit, ut posset esse certamen et aliqua in spectaculo gratia. Sic Deus, &c. .... Si desit hostis et pugna, nulla victoria est.....' Virtue is made perfect 'de malorum conflictatione .... Ergo diversitas est, cui omnis ratio veritatis innititur ....' The fall of man is in reality an ascent: knowledge of good, as well as of evil, was given simultaneously: 'Qua percepta, statim de loco sancto pulsus est, in quo malum non est .... relegatus in hunc communem orbem ut ea utraque simul experiretur. Quamdiu in solo Bono fuit, vixit ille princeps generis humani velut infans boni et mali nescius.' (See SCHELLING's *De Origine Mali.*) On this mediety of man depends both *intellectual* and *moral* worth, his peculiar dignity 'ut ratio virtutis sapientiaeque constaret, ... inter utrumque medium, ut haberet licentiam vel mali vel boni sequendi.' —Epit. 29 *Fit ut bonum sine malo esse non possit.*—De Ira 13 *Deus proposuit ei et bona et mala, quia sapientiam dedit, cuius omnis ratio in discernendis malis et bonis sita est. .... Invicem sibi alterutra connexa sunt, ut sublato alterutro utrumque sit tolli necesse .... positis tantummodo in conspectu bonis, quid opus est cogitatione, intellectu, scientia, ratione?* § 15 *Jam superius explanari simul Deum proposuisse bonum et malum (et bonum quidem diligere, malum autem .... odisse); sed ideo malum premisisse, ut et bonum emicaret: quod alterum sine altero (sicut saepe docui) intelligimus constare non posse.*

The difficulties and inconsistencies which arise afterwards in this dogma have their origin in the fluctuation between the *physical* and *moral*, the *impersonal* and *personal* conceptions. And it may here be remarked that the old feud of religion and philosophy (*Religio : Sapientia*) among the ancient Greeks may be traced to the same ambiguity. The extreme emphasis on capricious *personality* in popular superstition leads in reaction to the complete elimination of will and purpose from the theology of reflecting men, and the search for a *metaphysical* unity takes the place of an inquiry into *moral* motives and sacrifices of propitiation. Excessive anthropomorphism of mythology is followed by Ionic hylozoism, and later by the postulate of τὸ θεῖον or νόησις νοήσεως, which has no human affinities. LACTANTIUS alternates between a *physical* theory of God's development by contraries, in which there is always a systoechy of higher and lower in nature (whence comes our virtue and vice, as we choose one or the other), and a purely *moral* notion of evil: IV. 25 (sin is not) *necessitatis* (= physical and inevitable), *sed propositi ac voluntatis.* VI. 23 *Mens est enim profecto quae peccat.* Similarly, the leaders of this great struggle sometimes retire into the background, leaving only antithetic forces of nature, or come into prominence as independent *moral* wills, as persons fighting for the possession of man. I shall first cite those passages in which the *physical* polarity of the universe is traced to natural and inevitable causes; and next, and in conclusion, those in which the Evil Spirit is described as *personal.* In the first it is clear that the responsibility is thrown back upon the Creator, Who thus perhaps ceases to be a *moral* governor, and becomes rather a delighted spectator of mimic warfare. In the second series the emphasis is laid on the *personality* of Satan; but it is impossible to acquit LACTANTIUS of the charge of colouring this with *physical* notions. The first set of quotations tends to make it doubtful if the Body is not the sole cause of sin; the second reminds us that the Spirit is free. But it may be plausibly urged that it is the diverse character of the Good and the Bad Spirit that entails this system of confronting opposites in creation. Even in the former group frequent traces of this view may be found.

II. 9. Above God placed *lucem perennem et superos et vitam perpetuam, et contra in terra, tenebras et inferos et mortem.* So East and West, or the gates and grave of light. Day is of God, as are *omnia quaecumque meliora sunt; nox autem quam occidens extremus induxit, eius scilicet quem Dei esse aemulum diximus.* Again: *Nox, quam pravo illi antitheo dicimus attributam.* Elements are diverse: *Duo igitur illa principalia inveniuntur, quo diversam et contrariam sibi habent potestatem; calor et humor.*

II. 12. *In ipsius autem hominis fictione illarum duarum materiarum, quas inter se diximus esse contrarias, ignis et aquae conclusit perfecitque rationem* . . . . *Ex rebus igitur diversis ac repugnantibus homo factus est, sicut ipse Mundus ex luce et tenebris, ex vita et morte; quae duo inter se pugnare in homine praecepit. Utriusque officia sunt, ut hoc quod est ex caelo et Deo, imperet; illud vero quod ex terra est et Diabolo, serviat.*—III. 6 *Ita quoniam ex his duobus constamus elementis, quorum alterum luce praeditum est, alterum tenebris* (part is given to knowledge, part to ignorance).—IV. 25 *Etenim cum constet homo ex carne et spiritu* . . . . *caro quoniam terrena est* . . . . *copulatum sibi spiritum trahit secum* (but he is careful in this passage, as noted above, to guard himself from a mere superficial, necessitarian view of evil, as in the Manichean system; sin is a matter of the will (*propositi ac voluntatis*).—VI. 22 *Itaque fecit omnia Deus ad instruendum certamen duarum rerum.*—VII. 4 *Quoniam homo ex rebus diversis ac repugnantibus configuratus est, anima et corpore, id est, caelo atque terra, tenui et comprehensibili, aeterno ac temporali, sensibili atque bruto, luce praedito atque tenebroso; ipsa ratio ac necessitas exigebat et bona homini proponi et mala.*—VII. 5. For at the creation of man GOD *spiritum suum terreno corpore induit et involvit, ut compactus ex rebus diversis ac repugnantibus bonum ac malum*

Subordinate Dualism.   183

caperet. . . . . Ergo quia virtutem proposuit homini Deus, licet anima et corpus consociata sunt; tamen contraria sunt, et impugnant invicem.—VII. 9 *Rerum Natura his duobus elementis, quae repugnantia sibi et inimica sunt, constat, igne et aqua* (one ascribed to heaven and the other to earth).—De Ira, 15 *Denique ipsum mundum ex duobus elementis repugnantibus et invicem copulatis esse concretum, igneo et humido . . . . Sic et nos ex duobus aeque repvgnantibus compacti sumus, animo et corpore, quorum alterum caelo ascribitur, quia tenue est et intractabile, alterum terrae, quia comprehensibile est; alterum solidum et aeternum est, alterum fragile atque mortale. Hinc existit in hominibus naturae suae depravatio.*—§ 19 *Sed quoniam compactus est, ut diximus e duobus, animo et corpore, in altero virtutes, in altero vitia continentur, et impvgnant invicem.*

It appears then as if it were matter that was evil: we have besides certain inconsistent passages like the following:— II. 11 *Illius est totum (= Dei) quicquid sumus.* Yet the Supreme Good concerns the soul alone: III. 9 *(Summum Bonum) ut solius animi sit, nec communicari possit cum corpore.*—V. 21 *Non perspiciunt altius vim rationemque hominis, quae tota non in corpore sed in mente est.*—VI. 17 *Nos autem Summum Bonum non referimus ad corpus, sed omne officium solius animae conservatione metimur.*—But again we have IV. 24 (reminding us of Theophylact's ὅτι οὐ φύσει ἁμαρτωλὸς ἡ σάρξ), Christ came in the flesh, *ut ostendat etiam carnem posse capere virtutem.* Yet their good is mutually exclusive: *Animi bona mala sunt corporis, id est, opum fuga, voluptatum interdictio, doloris mortisque contemptus. Ita corporis bona mala sunt animi. . . . . Qui mavult bene vivere in aeternum, male vivit ad tempus et afficitur omnibus molestiis et laboribus.*—VII. 10 *Sicut duae vitae propositae sunt homini, quarum altera est animae, altera corporis; ita et mortes duae.*—VII. 12 (Platonic theory of the fall of the Soul) *Quia tenebroso domicilio terrenae carnis inclusa est* (so also De Ira, 1).—De Ira, 10 *Cui particulam de Sua sapientia dedit, et instruxit eum ratione, quantum fragilitas terrena capiebat.*

§ 19. The soul's goods, which consist *in continendis libidinibus contraria sunt corpori; et corporis bona, quae sunt in omni genere voluptatum, inimica sunt animo.* § 20 *Adeo subiecta est peccato fragilitas carnis, qua induti sumus.*

There are here confused traces of three different versions of the origin of Evil : (1) The 'Platonic' (as it is called), which is clearly restated by PLUTARCH (*de Is. et Osir.*) that matter coexists with God, and can be only imperfectly brought under discipline by His persuasion ; (2) that evil (or the possibility of it) is necessary from the configuration of the universe and Man, the microcosm, by an Almighty power, Who expresses Himself by opposites (*physical*); (3) that the world indeed is created entirely good (or, perhaps more accurately, indifferent), but the Evil Spirit and Man's Free-will find means of perverting its use to their own hurt.

We must now review those passages, which refer to the creation of Free Spirits (noting whether here, too, the complete independence of the *personal* is really preserved, and whether the character of the bad, as well as of the good, spirit is not a direct creation of God). As to the real hostility of this evil power to God, there is no doubt, whatever its cause. II. 1. The ingratitude of men, whence can it come, unless there be *aliquam perversam potestatem, quae veritatis semper sit inimica, quae humanis erroribus gaudeat, cui unum ac perpetuum sit opus, offundere tenebras et hominum caecare mentes, ne lucem videant, ne denique in caelum aspiciant.*—III. 29. As we Christians know that Fortune is nothing at all, *ita scimus esse pravum et subdolum spiritum, qui sit inimicus bonis* . . . . *qui contraria facit quam Deus.*—And thus a wilful rebel will be eternally punished : VII. 26 *perpetuo igni cremabitur in aeternum.* II. 17. He who yields to his evil advice *in illa decidet, quae in distributione rerum attributa esse ipsi malorum principi disputavimus, in tenebras scilicet et inferos et supplicium sempiternum.*

But in the following passages the *responsibility* of the Devil

Subordinate Dualism.

is by no means clear, and a certain physical necessity seems to overpower the unbiassed free-will: (but if Satan be a mere agent of the divine will, the question put in Hom. XX will press upon us for solution.) II. 8. Before God began the creation of the world, *produxit similem sui spiritum, qui esset virtutibus Dei patris praeditus . . . . Deinde fecit alterum in quo indoles divinae stirpis non permansit.* Tainted with the poison of his own envy, *suo arbitrio (quod illi a Deo liberum datum fuerat) contrarium sibi nomen ascivit . . . . Invidit enim illi antecessori suo, qui Deo patri perseverando . . . . carus est. Hunc ergo* ex bono per se *malum effectum Graeci* διάβολον *appellant, nos criminatorem vocamus, quod crimina in quae ipse illicit, ad Deum deferat.* But the interpolator is bolder: he begins the discussion by the statement: 'Fecit in principio bonum et malum'; and attempts to explain Satan's fall: 'Cur autem iustus Deus talem *voluerit* esse (explicabo). Fabricaturus Deus hunc Mundum, qui constaret ex rebus inter se contrariis atque discordibus, constituit ante diversa, fecitque ante omnia duos fontes rerum sibi adversantium, inter seque pugnantium; illos videlicet duos spiritus, rectum atque pravum, quorum alter est Deo tanquam dextra, alter tanquam sinistra, ut in eorum essent potestate contraria illa, quorum mixtura et temperatione Mundus . . . . constaret.' It will be seen that the interpolator, in the interests of the doctrine of omnipotence, leans to an entirely physical interpretation of evil.

'Quoniam fas non erat, ut a Deo proficisceretur malum (neque enim contra se ipse faciet); illum constituit malorum inventorem, quem cum faceret, dedit illi ad mala excogitanda ingenium et astutiam, ut in eo esset et voluntas prava, et perfecta nequitia; et ab eo contraria virtutibus suis voluit oriri, eumque secum contendere, utrumne ipse plus bonorum daret, an ille plus malorum. Sed rursus, quoniam Deo summo repugnari non potest, bonorum suorum potestatem illi ultori (*or* alteri) assignavit, quem supra bonum et perfectum esse diximus. Ita duos ad certamen composuit et instruxit, sed eorum alterum dilexit, ut bonum filium, alterum abdicavit, ut malum. (The angels too are formed to be his ministers 'unius sed repugnantis naturae; cf. *De Ira*, 15. Some remained good, others fell, but in the beginning all were 'pares aequa conditione apud Deum,' which is inconsistent with the description of the Devil just given.) 'Cum autem Deus ex his duobus alterum bono praeposuisset, alterum malo, exorsus est fabricam Mundi, omnibus his quos creavit ministrantibus et per certa officia dispositis.' (When therefore we read 'pars . . . . perversa voluntate descivit,' we feel there is an intrusion of an alien idea. 'Who doth resist His will?')—In LACTANTIUS himself, II. 9, the night is given to the *pravus Antitheus*; and II. 14, we have *cui ab initio dederat terrae potestatem.*—V. 22 *Deo quia repugnari non potest, ipse adversarios nomini suo excitat, non qui contra ipsum demum pugnent, sed contra milites eius.*—VI. 6 *Fons autem bonorum Deus est, malorum vero ille scilicet Divini nominis semper inimicus.* Opif. 19; (The interpolator explains the Devil's origin from the *moral* nature of man : 'Dedit ei et constituit adversarium nequissimum et fallacissimum spiritum, cum quo in hac terrestri vita sine ulla securitatis requie dimicaret. Cur autem Deus hunc vexatorem generis humani constituerit, breviter exponam. Ante omnia diversitatem voluit esse (ideoque vulgo non aperuit veritatem, sed eam paucissimis revelavit); quae diversitas omne arcanum Mundi continet . . . . Noluit enim Deus hominem ad illam immortalem beatitudinem delicato itinere pervenire. Daturus ergo virtutem, dedit hostem prius, qui animis hominum cupiditates et vitia immitteret; qui esset auctor errorum malorumque omnium machinator, ut quoniam Deus hominem ad vitam vocat, ille contra . . . . traducat ad mortem.'

Virtue is conceived of as mere impassible refusal to yield to the pains or pleasures of life, which be it noticed, VI. 4, it is God and not the Devil who puts in our path : VI. 18 *Summa igitur virtus habenda patientia est, quam ut caperet homo iustus, voluit illum Deus . . . . pro inerte contemni.*—VII. 5 *Ut pro-*

poneret homini virtutem, id est, tolerantiam malorum ac laborum, per quam posset praemium immortalitatis adipisci. Epitome, § 34 *Virtus enim malorum sustinentia est.*

For God desires us to reach our prize with difficulty, VII. 5 *Excogitavit . . . . inenarrabile opus quemadmodum infinitam multitudinem crearet animarum, quas primo fragilibus et imbecillis corporibus illigatas constitueret inter bonum malumque medias, ut constantibus ex utrisque naturis virtutem proponeret, ne immortalitatem delicate assequerentur ac molliter* (see Opif. 19, interpol.) *sed ad illud aeternae vitae ineloquibile praemium summa cum difficultate ac magnis laboribus pervenirent.*

From these passages it is clear that both Lactantius and his interpolator (somewhat bolder than the original author) fix their eyes on the *moral* life of man, and in explaining the universe start therefrom. Agreeing with the Stoics in the belief that the 'good will' is alone of value (that state of mind, ἀπάθεια, *quae nec eripi cuiquam, nec transferri in alterum potest* VII. 26), they reach instinctively two necessary corollaries :—(i) This good will is purely negative, and consists in denying all the messages of sense, and defying the blows of fortune; that is, life is to be entirely ascetic and unsocial in the midst of a world, which, made by God, is yet governed by the Devil; (ii) the powerlessness of the good will here, and yet the consciousness that it alone is of worth, requires a reward in a future life, to be won with difficulty at the price of the rejection of the insidious blandishments of the present. And though they do not face the question of the Devil's happiness in Hell, it is clear that this being does not possess free-will in the sense that we do, inasmuch as he and the world he governs were created for our probation, to represent a particular temptation. The Clementines, with a somewhat subtler inquiry, finally relieve him of responsibility by showing that his *physical* conformation entails this delight, either in evil or the punishment of the wicked, and this enjoyment of darkness and fire, as his natural abode. The final result of both authors, though it is one from which they seem to shrink, is that the world centres round personal and responsible man; that he is free to choose present or future life; and that the Lords of these two spheres are creatures and agents of God, who perform His will on the left hand and on the right, and are in a strict sense not free, for they do but execute His commands by an inherent law of their being. Such at least, if we can reduce scattered references to order, would seem to be the lesson conveyed by the Clementine writings and by the last Latin author before the Council of Nice; and if we recall the opposite views then current, *necessitarian* and *impersonal*, and remember that in course of time these views will find admission into the Christian Church itself, we shall find instruction in this honest attempt to approach *speculation* only from the *practical* point of view; to subordinate inconsistencies of result to the supreme importance of maintaining the dignity and the freedom of man the individual, and to regard the question of future life with no impartial coolness, but with a firm conviction that God is and that He is the rewarder of them that diligently seek Him. But it must be allowed that in these systems the mystery of Iniquity is by no means explained, nor the personal responsibility of the prince of evil. It seems to vanish behind *physical* language, and the notion of *rebel* finally gives way to that of *accredited agent*. Yet it may be safely said that none who attempt a final solution of this insoluble problem can afford to neglect these two points, in which the merit of the pseudo-Clementines and Lactantian writings is conspicuous: a firm adherence to the *righteous* and *personal* conception of God (at least so far as *human* responsibility is concerned, in distinction to *diabolic*), and a firm belief in the *freedom* of man and his discipline by the adversity and temptation of this present life.

www.ingramcontent.com/pod-product-compliance
Lightning Source LLC
Chambersburg PA
CBHW032007220426
43664CB00005B/169